Clairvoyant Secrets

Una Power

BLACKWATER PRESS

Printed in Ireland at the press of the publishers 1994

Editor
Antoinette Higgins

Design & Layout
Edward Callan

Cover
Philip Ryan

ISBN 0 86121 610 5

© – Una Power 1994

Produced in Ireland by
Blackwater Press
c/o Folens Publishers,
8 Broomhill Business Park,
Tallaght, Dublin 24.

Contents

1. Beginnings 7

2. How It All Works 15

3. Searching 25

4. Love 31

5. Money 40

6. Health 53

7. Work 64

8. Magical Places 76

9. Are You Psychic? 81

10. Psychic Power 87

Foreword

In this book I am taking the reader into the world of the clairvoyant. I describe what it is like to be clairvoyant, how it all began for me and describe some of the events in my clairvoyant career. Everyone who comes to me for a reading is treated in the strictest confidence. So, although I describe various people who came to consult me, I have made slight alterations in each case that I discuss to protect the real identity of the person. Towards the end of the book I describe fully three specific cases, but I asked permission of the people prior to writing and they all agree to be mentioned in this book. I hope you enjoy reading this book as much as I enjoyed writing it.

Una Power
October 1994

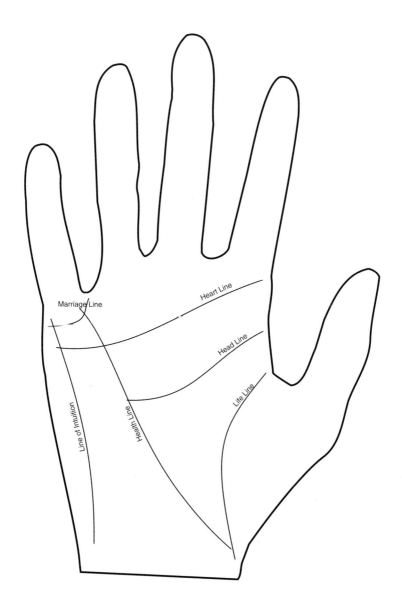

Chapter One

Beginnings

I had to learn how to read cards, it took a long time, but it has proved well worth it. Often I am asked if clairvoyance runs in the family. The answer is, no, it does not. Romanies and travelling people believe that clairvoyance belongs solely within their own race, this is not true. Anyone, I believe, can learn how to read cards and learn all about hand shapes and lines, but the ability to see into the future is something a person is born with irrespective of race. Incidentally, I have done palms and cards for travelling women and girls and have come to have the greatest respect for these hard-working girls and loyal wives.

My father was a great card player and used to love card games with the family. My three brothers at some stage or other were all keen card players, but I used to get bored and unable to concentrate. After a while I realised that I was seeing cards in a very different way to the rest of the family. I was noticing patterns that kept recurring.

There is a fabulous public library in Bristol and when I was about twelve I took out a book on card reading written by a woman described as the 'greatest seer on earth'. It was about tarot cards, cards with mystical pictures and odd inscriptions. It frightened me a bit as I thought some of the symbols were pagan or even evil. The card representing the devil was hideous; the card showing a skeleton depressed me; the collapsing tower I felt was menacing. The greatest seer on earth baffled and confused me so I returned the book to the library and tried to make out card meanings by myself.

Even if a person says they know nothing whatsoever about cards this is probably not true because an ordinary deck of playing cards is something we are all culturally familiar with. We know that hearts mean love, that clubs are to do with money and business, and that spades are generally unpleasant cards. What I believe happens during a card reading is that the enquirer subconsciously knows everything that is going to happen in the future and arranges the cards accordingly. I have the ability to read and understand the cards.

A friend of one of my brothers used to come to our house a lot and whenever he shuffled and dealt the cards he nearly always turned up the seven and eight of spades first. This intrigued me. Quite suddenly it came to me one day that those cards meant depression. From then on I used to watch closely. Although he never had a nervous breakdown, he was often depressed and moody.

Newspaper and magazine articles on the subject of card-reading fascinated me and I devoured them. Also I would shuffle the cards on a Sunday evening and lay them out in sets of three, jotting down on a piece of paper what I thought they meant. A week later I would check to see if I was right. By patience and learning I gradually learned the language of the cards. Each card is like a letter in the alphabet. In combination the cards have different meanings, alter that combination around and a very different meaning comes up. The letters D,O,G, spell dog. Alter them slightly and those letters spell God which is a completely different meaning. That is the way cards work.

Clairvoyance is the power to see things about people and the future not normally perceptible to the ordinary five senses. Second sight, or sixth sense, is a very good way to describe it. I have often thought of it as a natural derivative of my own five senses, because I use them too when doing a card and palm reading for a person.

Personally, I loathe the expression fortune-teller because it smacks of the fairground, women in ridiculous theatrical clothes with rolling eyes and strange predictions. I am none of those things. I was born in Bristol, the eldest of four children, went to university there and lectured at third level for fifteen years in social science. In most respects it was a pretty average upbringing in post-war Britain. What made me different was the fact that I was born clairvoyant, and knew as early as five that I had this special gift.

My godfather, a big man with a lilting Cork accent, came to visit us when his merchant ship docked in Bristol's port. He and my father sat down to talk of home – Ireland – while my mother made pots of tea and soda bread. When he left I ran out after him to say a special goodbye.

'Why did you do that?' my mother asked.

'Because we'll never see him again.'

A week later he drowned at sea.

My mother believed I had the gift of clairvoyance given to me when I received the Last Rites as a tiny baby only a few days old. 'If anyone lives after being given the Last Rites, I think God gives them a very special gift. He gave you clairvoyance.' But my father feared it. 'Devil's work', he called it.

So my gift had to be kept secret. Pity in a way, because I had discovered an amusing game to while away rainy winter Saturdays. I would look through the racing pages of my father's newspaper and pick out horses I thought would win in the afternoon. At five o'clock we would all sit down to tea and listen to the sports results on the wireless. Normally I would get four out of six winners. If I got all six my younger brother, Roger, had to give me his share of the plum jam. I was very bossy!

My father was not alone in believing that clairvoyance was some devil-given legacy, and one leading Irish journalist described me as 'unsettlingly witchlike'. The fault lies in a misconception that clairvoyance is something to do with the occult – a power given and driven by evil. That is all nonsense.

As a child I accepted my gift as entirely normal, as a part of me, just like having another sort of memory, as a property of my brain. That belief has sustained me throughout life.

Religious Conflict

When I am doing a card and palm reading I am aware of a tremendous surge of physical energy radiating through my body. My temperature rises and my mind is very, very clear. As I touch a person's palm, and trace their lines of life, love, and head, I can feel a buzzing and tingling in my fingertips. Images shape in my mind and thoughts enter my head. Last year a well-dressed middle-aged woman came to me for a reading. For a brief instant I saw a nun's veil on her head.

'You are a nun.'

Her face relaxed. 'I was wondering if you would know that. I left the convent a few weeks ago and need your advice on what I am going to do with the rest of my life.'

At the end of the reading she asked me if clairvoyance conflicted with my Catholicism as it was stated in the Bible that the art of prophecy was a sin. That question coming from the nun was simple and based on curiosity, and I had no problem explaining that I felt no conflict at all as clairvoyance was only a problem if it became a substitute for religion. It was a deeply offensive question when put to me by a ranting Charismatic, propped up by hair gel and idiocy, who came to the radio station, where I produce and present a nightly programme, to attack me because I gave some clairvoyant readings one evening on the air.

It was done that evening for fun, for a few people who rang in. I stopped it because the phone lines were jammed with callers wanting readings and because of a situation in which I told a young woman caller that there were two men in her life and that she should take care as a pregnancy was likely. After the programme she rang again and said she bitterly regretted speaking to me live on air because her husband was also listening to the conversation on his car radio. She had been having an affair outside her marriage and was about to give birth to her first child! Dangerous stuff, messing frivolously with people's lives. I take my clairvoyance very seriously and always use it to help people whenever possible.

We live in an age when people make predictions all the time. We want to know about tomorrow's weather, population trends over the next few years, election forecasts and when recession will end. I am just another forecaster, that is all.

Common Sense

When I am doing a reading I use my five senses to observe the person, how they move, sit, deal the cards, dress, make eye contact. The voice is important as most women talk like their mother and most men copy their father. That gives me clues about upbringing. A harsh, rasping voice usually belongs to an insensitive person, while a soft, hesitant voice belongs to a person bullied as a child. Anxiety is the most difficult of all emotions to conceal and it shows in the eyes and voice.

The touch of a person's hand tells me a great deal about their current emotional state. A hot palm denotes anxiety and tension, while a cool one belongs to a person with few emotional problems and sometimes little tender feelings. Smell is the most powerful of the senses and I am acutely sensitive to it. Someone drenched to the eyebrows with perfume or after-shave usually has something emotional to hide, some aspect of personality they fear to have exposed. Although I cannot taste a person – contrary to some people's belief I do not actually eat people – I substitute colour for it.

Colour

Colour is very important to psychics as colours influence mood and can enhance or destroy a person's quality of life. When I was lecturing in Bristol, and then here in Ireland, I could tell pretty quickly which students were likely to succeed at the end of the course by the colours they wore. Girls who wore pink were always successful in college and later in their career. Boys who chose grey were sloggers academically and later chose very safe careers. Incidentally black, one of my favourite colours, is often chosen to conceal a strong and dominant personality.

Psychic Energy

Sometimes people want to tape a reading and I unfortunately cannot allow them to do this because the energy I generate during a reading interferes with the tape recorder, and even more unfortunately, with the electrical apparatus in my cottage in the lovely Kildare countryside.

One journalist who came to interview me was sceptical about this and insisted that a tape recorder was switched on. A few minutes later she was startled (and I hope impressed) when the toaster in the kitchen switched itself on and popped up! A photographer found his lighting system flashed and flickered bizzarely until I left the room as he was photographing me doing a reading. I have no explanation, for this phenomenon other than the one I have already given. I simply accept that it happens.

Princess Diana

Clairvoyance is a strange and scarcely understood gift. It has been examined by the various psychical research societies, but along with spiritualism, hauntings, water divining and levitation, so that thinking about it has become muddled and it is associated with the credulous and deluded. There are times when I cannot understand it myself. Sometimes when I look at a person it is as though a mask has slipped off their face and I see things about their personality that are not normally projected.

Princess Diana was on the television, and as it seemed to me, simpering and whining about her ills and ails, with not a dry eye in the house. Quite suddenly, I saw her with a face of cunning and manipulation laughing behind tear-filled eyes. There came to me the instant conviction that she would never sit on the throne of England. When I voiced these impressions on air, and later in an article in a leading Irish Sunday newspaper, I got a massive and extremely hostile reaction from seemingly Royalty-crazed Irish public. A year later her private secretary went public and said much the same thing. The impression that Princess Diana will never occupy the English throne is not confined to me!

Auras

Quite often I can detect an aura around a person. It is never very clear, and the impression of colour only lasts a few seconds, but it does tell me something about the character and temperament of the person. A young Canadian was sent by a mutual friend for a reading.

'He's badly in need of your advice, Una. The poor guy has been accused of doing away with his wife to get her money. Her death was an accident. He wants to know if he should sue the silly woman who is slandering him.'

He parked his car at the end of the laneway to my cottage and walked up to me with all the sexless grace of a dim-witted athlete. Baby-blue eyes shone in a deeply tanned face. He was framed in the doorway and I squinted up at him, my eyes momentarily blinded by the strong sun. An aura emanated around him, black and flashed with red, denoting hatred and anger.

'Una Power?' I felt menace in his voice.

'She's been called away to Dublin, I'm looking after the house.'

His mouth tightened, he looked like the school bully cheated of a victim. Without a word he turned and loped off down the laneway. Presently I heard the roar of a powerful car engine and as it receded into the far distance I felt myself trembling as though I had had a very lucky escape. At times like that I wonder if my gift is a blessing or a curse.

Chapter Two

How it all works

There is a misconception that the type of person to consult a clairvoyant is a lovesick young girl wanting to know when will the tall, dark stranger appear in her life. There are, naturally, some young girls who come to me because they want to know about their love lives, but most people who want a reading have a specific query for which they need an answer. In the main, three times as many women come as men, but all are perfectly serious. It might be a crisis in a marriage, or the need to know when, or if, a house will be sold. Changing jobs in Ireland at a time when jobs are scarce and firms closing down is a major decision, and one not lightly made.

I would normally expect people to use their logical faculties in decision making. But sometimes logic fails and a psychic point of view and a peep into the future is no harm at all.

Years ago a girl who would then have been about twenty-eight came to me for a reading. She was in love with her boss who spent every Tuesday night with her. He had promised that one day he would leave his wife and live permanently with the mistress he alleged to love. Only that his wife was a sick woman, he had said, he would have done it on the instant. Over the years I have been quite staggered by the number of sick wives in Ireland! The girl was trembling with love for this man, it spilled all over her, blotting out everything else. She wanted to know so badly that one day they would be together that I felt if I did not tell her that this would be so she might have a breakdown.

She had no marriage line, and her cards showed an ace and eight of spades – a clear and unequivocal NO. Feeling that fool's hope was better than no hope I told her that one day she and her lover would be together.

She was forty-five when I saw her again. For once, the man in such a case as this was telling the truth, and his wife did die of her illness. But within six months he had married a girl of thirty and was starting another family. In the meantime, thanks to me, the faithful mistress had waited patiently through all her fertile years, with no hope at all of meeting a man who would love and honour her openly and give her his name, his time and his children. From then on I decided that in the future I would always be truthful in readings, even if it hurt or disappointed the person at the time. Hurt fades, there is always hope, and when the cards show a problem, they also show a solution.

Cards

If I see the ace of hearts and the seven of hearts together I know that means the birth of a baby girl. Then I look for other cards to tell me if the birth is about to take place, or has already taken place. My own clairvoyance tells me to whom the birth relates. A priest came for a reading and the birth cards appeared. By elimination it was not meant for him as being a priest he had taken a vow of celibacy, therefore it had to be someone close to him. The ten of clubs, the card of travel, was beside the birth cards, followed by the queen of clubs, a dark haired woman.

'You are going on a journey to a dark-haired woman who is pregnant. She is going to have a daughter.'

He grinned. 'Doubt it. I am going to Armagh tomorrow to stay with my sister. She has six grown up boys and at her age, she's forty-seven, I don't think there'll be any more wains.'

A month or so later I got a call from a woman in Armagh who was that priest's sister.

'My brother told me of your prediction to give me a laugh. I thought I'd started the change but went along for a check-up anyway.' Her voice shook, I was not sure if she was laughing or crying. 'I was stuck to the floor when the doctor told me I was four months pregnant.'

Although I never heard from her, or him, again I am sure she gave birth to a fine healthy child five months later.

A person does not have to believe in the cards in order to have a reading. The meanings remain the same whatever the enquirer thinks or feels. But it is important to me that the enquirer says very little. I prefer to read what I see before me, only asking questions if I am unsure of something. For instance, the eight and nine of clubs together can either mean a promotion at work or passing an exam. Unless I am quite sure, I usually ask which is more likely to be the case.

The cards of value between two and six, inclusive, I discard, and simply deal with the remaining thirty-two cards. The complex language and many variations of the cards no longer puzzles me because I have mastered it, but it has never lost its power to intrigue and fascinate me.

During a reading I look at the palm and lay out the cards simultaneously. By touching the cards and the palm lines I forge a psychic link enabling me to get names of countries, place names, occupations, or to see pictures clearly in my mind of the sort of things revealed in the cards. While I do not ask people to suspend their critical faculties during a reading, I do ask them to be patient with matters in the cards that appear obscure or irrelevant to them.

When someone comes for a reading I make them make an appointment, I never, ever see anyone without an appointment. That means I can have a few minutes to meditate quietly first, this prepares my mind. Readings take place in the study where it is calm and quiet. Each person is seen individually. I cannot concentrate on a person if a friend sits in with them. Neither, under those circumstances, can the enquirer be frank enough.

We all have secrets, even from best friends.

We sit on either side of a small desk. While the enquirer is shuffling the deck of cards I jot down their date of birth, just the day and month and add those numbers across. For example the twenty-sixth of November, is 26, 11. Added across that adds up to ten, 10, adding the double number together gives one. Over the years I have worked out my own little personality scale based on this system which gives numbers one to nine. It is very simple. The odd numbers tend to belong to people with scientific, analytical personalities, the business-like types, those with high energy and organised lives. The number one personality has most of these qualities, which decrease as the scale goes down to nine. Nines are often extremely hard-working, but something of the loner exists in the personality. The even numbers tend to be creative, artistic and sociable. The two's are kind and usually have a balanced, surly nature. Going down the scale to the eight's they become slightly more emotional and eight's often suffer from bouts of depression or have an acute reaction to a family row, or loss of employment.

A Limerick lady came to me for a reading, she wanted to know about her business prospects as she was thinking of opening a shop. The cards at the head of the layout were a grouping of spades, the ace and the nine, meaning death. Most people think that the ace of spades alone means death. It does not. The ace of spades standing alone often indicates a new business venture, while the ace of spades and ace of clubs is always a contract. In the Limerick lady's case the death cards were followed by the ten of spades, a card of ill-omen, indicating that the death would be in some way unfortunate. The knave of spades followed the ten. Certainly the death was shocking in some way. A king, queen and knave of hearts followed indicating that it would be that of a man, woman and child.

As I looked at the cards I touched the woman's palm lines

and felt great kindness and compassion in her. Keeping very still and quiet I tried to focus my mind on the cards to clarify the picture but I could see nothing more. All I felt after a few minutes intense concentration was a message for the woman to go to the family involved when the death occurred, as her visit would be of great importance to them. She found her reading obscure to the point of nonsense and said so. When she left she was very disappointed having travelled a long way to see me. My own feeling was of disappointment too, and a feeling that I had failed.

Shortly afterwards, a priest, a young mother, and her child were all murdered in the West of Ireland and I knew instantly that was the death I had seen in the cards. My Limerick lady returned for another reading and to tell me that she knew the family of the man who had been involved with the crimes and that she had gone to them. She was glad she had because their suffering was every bit as great as that of the relatives of the dead people.

Hands and Palms

Naturally I would look for support for this in the hands of the enquirer. The shape and colour of the hand is as important as the lines on the palm. What I like about palms is their individuality, their uniqueness. The palms and lines in them belong entirely and exclusively to the owner.

'Don't tell me anything bad.' People often say.

I can understand that attitude. It is perfectly normal. People want hope and good news, not a dreary catalogue of things to come. When something unpalatable appears in the cards I phrase it in such a way so that the enquirer can deal with it as positively as possible. The head line, that is the line running across the centre of the palm from the base of the life line, indicates how well able the enquirer is to deal with the truth. A straight, deeply grooved head line indicates clear and logical thinking. One that is slightly curved down is associated with an artistic personality while one that slopes sharply down the hand belongs to a person with a depressive nature. The latter type is likely to brood exclusively on bad news without balancing it by either a solution to a difficult problem, or by any good news in the reading.

Palm shape is important as it is my first guide to the type of person sitting before me. Slender hands with a lot of lines belong to the thinker, the person working with their brain and applying a body of learned theory to practical situations; like a doctor or a solicitor. A big square hand belongs to the practical creator, someone involved in cooking, sculpting, painting or carpentry. Bony knuckles belong to physically active people who like making money.

Watch out for the person with a fleshy hand, reddish in colour and warm to the clasp - this person has a highly sexual nature.

Very pale palms often indicate a person with a physical weakness, maybe lack of iron. Real sickness is indicated by a faint, or patchy life line. But more of that later.

The most important part of the hand is the thumb because that tells me very quickly just what sort of thinking and emotional attitudes the person has. Several people I know involved in film or programme making have remarkably similar thumbs. All are long and flexible with a square shaped bone at the end. Thumbs that turn outward when the palm is placed face up on the table are flexible in their thinking and good, honest communicators. Where the thumb is inflexible and will not turn outward the person has a very private, possibly even a secretive nature and takes a lot of time to change their mind or opinion about things. Thumbs that curve backwards in an arc when the thumb is extended denote a person with a happy, pliant nature, always willing to see the other persons point of view.

Readings generally last about twenty minutes, sometimes longer if necessary. It is quite pointless to babble on for an hour, repeating oneself over and over again. It bores people and does not enlighten them at all. Quite often I am asked how long readings take, and sometimes people are disappointed hoping to sit with me for an hour. An hour would be a therapy session. And, I do not get more clairvoyant as minutes tick on.

Astrology

There is tremendous therapeutic value in a clairvoyant session. It is exclusively about the enquirer and his or her concerns. There are often unusual insights gained into the personality or situation currently concerning them that they might not have seen in normal circumstances. I have often thought that the real value of consulting an astrologer is the pure indulgence hearing oneself discussed, usually in glowing terms!

As a teenager it was wonderful to read all about Sagittarians (my sign) and what fantastically wonderful people we were. Marvellous fun, full of life and vitality! I swallowed every word quite uncritically. It might have been stupid, but it did give my ego a boost.

As I got older I realised the nonsense in believing that a girl born in a shanty town in South Africa on precisely the same date and time as a girl on a Mayo farm would have the same character, personality and life chances. It is our culture, economic disposition, religious influences which shape us and our lives. The description of the typical Saggitarian girl was that she walked upright, loved the outdoors, had fair skin and reddish hair, and veered towards a career in journalism or teaching. I was staggered by the aptness of the description - that was me to the letter. A very brief study of the map showed me that the world was three quarters black or coloured, how could that description be applied generally? It could not. That does not invalidate astrology, but it does limit it to the white Western world, and even more narrowly to the middle classes. But it is fun and, if a person wants to sit with a good astrologer for a couple of hours discussing their own personality, it can be helpful. Many people find the study of astrology a fascinating and worthwhile pursuit.

A girl once wrote to me via my magazine column expressing disappointment that her boyfriend was unkind and physically vicious to her because of his horoscope sign – and wondering if he would ever change. I felt some sort of despair at the ignorance and credulity behind such a letter. It is quite wrong to say 'I'm like this because of my astrological sign and can't change'. That sort of thinking brings the whole range of psychic activities into disrepute, as it implies a set of fixed laws governing implacably our future. This cannot be true, and if it is, then it entirely contradicts the notion of free will.

Free Will

Free will, freedom, the ability and opportunity to make our own choices is one of our most precious and hard won liberties. It is, I believe, morally and intellectually wrong to say, 'I have no choice'. When I lay out the cards and it shows, perhaps, the two black aces and the seven of clubs, indicating a house move, the enquirer is still at liberty not to move home.

That particular combination of cards shows the signing of a property contract. A Carlow man came to me for a reading to find out when the contracts giving him ownership of the house he was living in with his wife and family would be signed. They had been renting the house from a couple living in Dublin and had decided to buy it as the Dublin couple wanted to sell. He had, informally, given them a deposit of five thousand pounds. That surprised me because Irish country people are generally extremely shrewd in all matters relating to land and property.

The cards showed the two black aces, the seven of clubs, but there then followed the eight of spades and the remaining three sevens. The eight of spades indicates the failure of the contract, or, that it would be unwise to sign. The three sevens show legal proceedings. My interpretation was that he should not sign the contract at all, and should seriously reconsider whether or not he and his family continued living in the house as there were likely to be legal difficulties ahead, but I did not know more. 'I want that house and no other.' He was adamant, and left.

A couple of months later his wife came to see me, a fraught little woman with the tight mouth of someone not allowed to voice her opinions much.

'I want you to look at the cards and tell me if we are going to get our money back, the house sale has fallen through.'

It transpired that her husband had gone to the couple and given them a further five thousand pounds to hurry the sale of the house. *His* interpretation of my reading, which he considered vague, was that the difficulties had been caused by himself. But the Dublin couple had separated and the wife was pregnant by another man. There existed a bitter conflict with little immediate hope of resolution and the wife wanted to claim the Carlow property as a family home. The husband wanted to sell the Carlow house, but not to his wife and her lover. The conflict has still not been resolved and, although the man and his family still live in the house, they do not own it, and have still not got their money back.

More About Cards

After the first reading of the cards – that is done in conjunction with the palm, the enquirer then deals the cards again. This time, instead of laying out all thirty cards in lines of three, the enquirer leaves them in three heaps on the desk. The first is the pile containing information about love, and family matters. The second pile is about money and career; the third is for health. After that I get the enquirer to select six cards at random from the pack this will show, in the case of an unmarried person, who they would be most compatible with, the colouring and disposition of the prospective partner, or, it can show financial prospects.

Finally, the enquirer shuffles the pack thinking of a wish they would like to come true. The cards are placed face down on the desk and cut once. I can then tell from the positioning of the wish card, the nine of hearts, whether or not the enquirer will get their wish I have always been struck by how often people wish, not for fame or fortune, but simply for happiness and contentment for themselves and their families. The pursuit of happiness and well-being is probably one of the most important of all aims for people I have read for. Maybe I have been exceptionally lucky in dealing with kind and caring people.

Chapter Three

Searching

There are some aspects of my work as a clairvoyant that I absolutely hate. One of these is when I am asked to search for a missing person. When a man or woman, or anyone for that matter, goes missing, the normal channels of search are used. The Gardai have a set of extremely sensible guidelines, and are pretty thorough in investigating everything, particularly if they feel that there is something suspicious about the disappearance. If they fail then friends and relatives can advertise in the newspapers, go out looking singly or in groups, ask questions, and make enquiries.

By the time family or friends get to me, it is because I am the end of the line even though that is not a good omen, I never, ever, turn them away.

One woman of about forty came to me to help find her daughter. At my request she brought a photograph of an attractive girl of sixteen or seventeen, and a black tee-shirt belonging to the girl. I brought the woman into my study where I read, write and do some preparation for my radio programme. The desk was cleared, I placed the photograph on it, invited the girl's mother to sit opposite me, and took out my crystal pendulum. Sometimes I use a silver pendulum but more often the crystal one which is suspended from a narrow silver chain.

Holding the end of the chain I allowed the crystal to hang motionless over the photograph. After a few seconds it moved quickly in a clockwise direction. A grateful sigh escaped me that meant the girl was alive. Her mother had not doubted that, she was just anxious to know where her daughter was.

Holding the tee-shirt in both hands I closed my eyes and set my mind free to track its owner down. There was an immediate and vivid sense of the girl being close, very close.

'She is not far away', I explained.

The woman had expressed a fear that her daughter had gone to England with an unsuitable and much older boyfriend. The cards – I use ordinary playing cards – showed that the girl was with a blond woman who was probably related to her. Although this puzzled me, it did not square with what I had already been told, I relayed this to the woman.

'I know who that is!', The woman got up and left looking much happier than when she arrived.

A few days later the girl in the photograph came to see me, she was furiously angry.

'You had no right to tell my mother where I was! The Guards knew where I was and they told my parents I was OK, but they wouldn't say where I was because I asked them not to.'

She got very red in the face as she spoke.

'Your mother was very concerned about you', she only wanted to know where you were. What harm is there in that?'

'My mother is an alcoholic and has done damn all for me for the last seventeen years. She knows that the old man abuses me and interferes with me and never lifts a finger to stop him. *That's* why I left home, I'm with my aunt and that's where I'm staying! And the next time you poke your nose into other people's lives, at least ask their permission first.'

She left without giving me a chance to tell her how very sorry I was about the mess. Of course, she was perfectly right and it taught me a lesson I was very careful to apply in the future. Next time such a search was instigated I got as many details as possible from the searcher before informing about a missing friend or relative.

Annie McCarrick

I got a telephone call from a softly-spoken American man. 'I'm
Annie McCarrick's uncle, she's missing. My sister, Annie's
mother, and I, would like to come to see you. We need your
help in locating Annie.'

Another thoughtless girl gone off on a jaunt, I thought,
without troubling to tell a soul. Probably a man in it
somewhere.

The mother and uncle agreed to motor down from Dublin
immediately and be with me an hour later. While waiting for
them I tried to recall the brief details I had read in the paper.
Annie McCarrick, a young American student, had left her
Dublin city flat to go to a beauty spot, Enniskerry, in the
Wicklow hills. Someone reported seeing her with a young man
in a public house in Enniskerry that evening and she had not
been seen since.

Annie McCarrick's uncle was a tall, studious looking man
with a gentle manner and troubled eyes. His sister, was small
and neat, looking like a kind school teacher. She had
photographs of Annie and a grey sweater belonging to her.
When she sat across from me at my desk she was quite
composed.

'I'm convinced Annie is alive. My instinct tells me that's so,'
she said.

Her brother sat back in his chair, looking down at the
photographs that I was studying. The room was full of his
sorrow. I was impressed by Mrs McCarrick's certainty because I
trust gut instinct and I often depend on the maternal one.

The photographs showed a healthy girl with frank eyes and a
wide trusting smile. This was no thoughtless brat off on the razz
with a boyfriend, but a kind and generous girl, probably a bit
naive and certainly emotionally younger than her twenty-six
years.

27

The pendulum hanging over the photograph stayed quite still for perhaps a minute, then moved sluggishly in an anti-clockwise direction. The air in the room was cold and I got the scent of earth in my nostrils. A dreadful wave of despair invaded me. Annie had certainly gone to Enniskerry that day and more certainly had never left it.

I could barely meet Mrs McCarrick's eyes.

'I'm so very sorry, but in my opinion, Annie is no longer alive.'

Annie's mother would not be convinced and clung to her belief that her daughter was alive. It is important to tell the truth in a reading, there is no worse hope than fool's hope. But maybe at that time Mrs McCarrick needed false hope before facing the dreadful truth. By then, I too had lost an only and dearly loved child and it is the most devastating and final of all things for a parent to bear. One is left to creep wounded through life for ever more.

We spent a long time talking, drinking tea, going over Annie McCarrick's childhood, upbringing and future hopes. But all the while I could feel her death and formed a picture in my mind of where her body lay. It was in some sort of box or pipe, partially underground and the view across from it was of mounds of earth. There were other things, too, like the impression that she had a row with someone, had been in tears, had gone to Enniskerry in willing hope to some assignation important to her.

Later, after the McCarricks had left, I was completely drained and exhausted. Psychic energy is like that, strong at the time, but leaving me physically depleted afterwards. After taking a rest I contacted a friend in the Gardai who confirmed for me many of the details I had picked up psychically. He relayed the description of the terrain I saw to a Guard familiar with the Enniskerry area, but it was the scene of building work. I believe it will be a very long time before Annie McCarrick's body is found.

To Bury the Dead

Even in deep tragedy families need a body to bury, they need a set time to begin official grieving, to carry on with their lives. A Wicklow family who came to see me had already accepted that their son was dead, he had drowned at sea. Experts had told them that the most likely place to find his body if it was washed ashore would be farther up the coast around Dublin or possibly Dun Laoghaire. Studying a map and using my pendulum I disagreed, pin-pointing a spot very close to where his boat had been found. The mother and sister wept on hearing this, but they were somewhat relieved to be able to continue their search. Then a strange thing happened. I got the strong impression of the dead man in the room. He was biggish, lively, with a quick temper and impish laugh. He passed a hand across his upper arms and chest and the words came into my mind, 'Tell them my rash is better.'

On the morning of his death his mother said she had gone to the chemist to buy some preparation for a rash on her son's arms and chest.

Another relative, a man, was called into the room to look at the spot I had indicated on the map. He shook his head.

'I doubt he's there, and if he is, he won't be found, it's a rocky and dangerous stretch of coast.'

'He will be found.' I had dealt the cards and, wishing that the young man's body would be found, turned up the nine of hearts – the wish card.

It was very thoughtful of the family to telephone me a few months later to tell me of the final outcome. A freak accident had driven an English yachtsman into the rocks on the Wicklow coast. Being unfamiliar with the coastline he did not know that it was dangerous until his vessel ran aground in shallow water. In that shallow, rock strewn inlet he saw a body. The Wicklow family had the small, but very important comfort, of knowing that they could bury the dead and sit by a graveside.

Fun Searches

There is another side to searching that is neither serious nor dramatic. Every week I have a psychic column in an Irish woman's magazine. People write in with a variety of psychic queries and I do my best to answer them. It is great fun and I enjoy it very much. One woman even wrote asking my psychic help in locating two lost skirts. Rings, documents, wills, in fact, *anything* of real or sentimental value I try to locate, sometimes with success, but not always. But, skirts? People are, sometimes, very odd.

Chapter Four

Love

Neither clairvoyance nor psychology can tell quite why we need love, only that when it is absent from our lives we are incomplete. Babies starved of love do not thrive as well as loved babies. Having someone to love gives our lives point and purpose and enables most of us to carry on dreary or tough jobs. Loving and being loved is a powerful source of energy and well-being. The loss of love, or a lover, is like a physical blow. There is a feeling of torment inside and the future looks bleak. No matter how successful a person is, or how wealthy, life without love has no flavour.

No matter what serious purpose or query brings an enquirer to me for a reading, nothing brings quite the smile of joy to a face as hearing that they are about to be loved. It always acts like a very powerful tonic. Sometimes, of course, a reading shows that the enquirers feelings are not, or will never be, returned. That is always disappointing news, but better to hear than raising false hopes.

To some people love simply means a good sexual experience. For others it means a chance to start a family. Some girls want marriage as a means of socially approved identity. Others need, and can give, that very special intimate sharing of mind, body and emotions. Some people are simply not cut out for this and should really never marry. Their marriages are doomed, if not to failure, to miserable sterility.

Face of Love

The ability to give and receive love are shown in the face, as is the propensity to infidelity. A long upper lip slightly protruding over the lower lip shows a person with passionate, sometimes ungoverned feelings. This sort of mouth is most likely to belong to the unfaithful type. A short upper lip indicates fidelity, devotion, and a sweet, pliant personality, one who will adapt readily to the compromises needed if the relationship is to succeed throughout the normal ups and downs of life.

Be very wary of a person who talks from the side of their mouth as they are practised liars. What is often hurtful for a partner involved with this type of person is that the lies are quite needless. A thrusting lower lip is a sign of a passionate nature; so, if you are not keen on sex, do not get involved, as you will only disappoint each other.

A small mouth belongs to someone who does not like making unnecessary conversation, and is happy to spend time with a partner in comfortable silence.

A quality of the man or woman with a long upper lip is the need to have a partner who depends on them. Therefore they should be looking for a partner with a short upper lip.

A very thin mouth is usually owned by a person who needs a lot of control in a relationship. They make decisions easily and quickly, but do not discuss or negotiate overmuch. That works fine if the partner is dependent or indecisive – and some people are just that. It is not a fault, merely a personality trait, and is perfectly compatible with the right partner. Very full lips show someone physically passionate and intellectual. They can be great fun to be with, but can become obsessive about relationships. A prospective partner – especially if the partnership is to be lifelong, should lay down some pretty definite ground rules about the expression of jealous tantrums!

Wide mouthed people are generous about love, they nurture and inspire with love. But they gab about it too.

There is a basic difference between men and women when it comes to communicating over important matters, like expressing emotional feelings of love, or grief, men tend to go silent and women need to talk and analyse. I have seen a lot of relationships founder over this. A couple grieving over the death of a child, or parent, seem to grow apart in mutual weariness and misunderstanding because the woman often does not understand that a man copes with his deepest feelings in silence. It does not mean that he does not have these feelings, merely that he is unable to express them. She often takes his silence as a rejection of her and she assumes that he is unwilling to listen to her or enter into her feelings. What she is practising is a form of dependency, not love.

Lovely eyes do not always mean a loving personality, unfortunately. Green eyes – which, incidentally, are usually associated with a psychic personality – belong to people most likely to flirt, or play mind games. But green, or hazel-eyed people are as capable as blue, grey or brown eyed people of loving faithfully and with commitment. Deeply sunken eyes often belong to the sort of person who enjoys analysing the emotional side of the relationship. They would be advised to steer clear of a partner with wide, well-opened eyes. Those eyes see, observe, record, but leave words unsaid.

Love Lines

The line that starts beneath the base of the little finger and arcs across the palm upwards towards the base of the index finger is the line of heart and emotion. The short horizontal line above it, directly beneath the little finger, is the marriage line. Having a marriage line does not automatically guarantee that a person will marry, but they will certainly have the chance.

When I am looking at the heart line, I study the colour, the shape, and heat or coolness from it. Sometimes when I lightly trace this line with my fingertip I can feel a buzz, like a small electrical charge. This always indicates that a new love interest is about to come into the person's life.

A smooth, unbroken line, curving upwards to the base of the index finger shows a person with everything most desired from a relationship and marriage before them. The emotional life will be uncomplicated, contented, whether or not they choose to marry or enter into a committed relationship.

A chained appearance, or breaks along the emotional line indicates an enquirer who will not find love an easy or rewarding business, unless they choose sensibly. When this line is faded, or cold, then the fire, and probably the friendship has gone out of the relationship. When the line shows patches of red, or feels hot, then there are usually rows taking place and the partnership is in an argumentative, even unreasonable phase. A short, straight heart line tells me that the person is brisk, efficient and controls emotions – what passionate emotions they have – with ease. This type of person would mate well with a similar sort of personality. It might be true that, initially, opposites attract, but they rarely turn into life-long, compatible relationships.

Cards of Love

There is only one combination of cards that shows real, true love and that is the seven and nine of hearts on either side of a court card. A very good-looking man came for a reading wanting to know if his wife was being unfaithful to him as she had changed and become withdrawn. The seven and nine of hearts appeared on either side of the queen of diamonds – a blond woman loved him.

'My wife is blond but if she loves me, she is not showing it. There was a firm's dinner last week and she just refused to come with me. She won't talk to me anymore. It's as though we've become two strangers.'

He was obviously deeply hurt and confused. His confusion was shared by me too. The two red eight's were on either side of the seven and nine of hearts. The blond woman loved her husband and was faithful to the marriage. I asked him to cut the cards again and take, at random, six cards for himself. He asked.

'Why do you want me to cut the cards?'

'Because I want to see if you love your wife.'

'I wouldn't be here if I didn't. You're my last hope.'

I privately thought this a rather dramatic view of the situation, but looked at the cards he had selected. Again the seven and nine of hearts appeared, he did love. But they were on either side of the nine of clubs – this man had fallen in love with his work. I looked at his palm and saw a vertical line beneath the index finger, the sign of compulsion, obsession. This man was a workaholic! There were diamonds, the cards of conversation, but they were grouped around the seven and eight of clubs, again the cards of work in this particular context. When he talked, which was often, it was all about his work. No wonder she did not want to go to the firm's dinner, she would have had another dose! We discussed this for a while and he was quite willing to accept that his work had taken over his life, and that when he and his colleagues on the newspaper he worked for got together they talked work all the time to the exclusion of everything else. They also, he admitted, talked to each other, excluding partners from the conversation. He did have, however, a basically receptive and friendly nature and a real anxiety to make his marriage work. I often think of that couple and others like them and wish them every happiness in their lives.

Infidelities

The two black eight's show infidelity. If those cards appear around a court card then that person is cheating on their partner. If there are any heart cards then the partner is engaged in a real relationship likely to threaten the marriage, or permanent relationship. I used to hate divulging this, but often it is a relief to a person to know that their fears and suspicions are correct.

'I don't like it one little bit', one young wife confessed. 'But he's told me so often that I'm imagining things and have a sick mind when I accuse him that I've actually started going to therapy to cure myself.'

No Hopers

It is incredibly difficult to convince a man or woman in love with someone who does not care for them, or will never care for them, that that is the case. If the ace of spades and eight of spades appear around a particular person that is a very definite No. I can remember trying really hard to convince a girl that the man she had her eye on would never fall in love with her, and that there was absolutely no hope of marriage with him. It would, quite simply, never, ever happen.

'But he told me he loves me and that I'm his best friend.'

'There is a difference between loving and being in love. You can love a friend, but it's very different to the sort of love you have with a sexual partner.'

It came to me quite suddenly as I looked at the cards around him what the root of the problem with him was.

'Could he be homosexual?'

She coloured from her forehead to her neck. It was something she had already suspected, I knew that.

'I don't care if he is, I know I can cure him.'

Oh, dear! There are times when I feel like shaking an enquirer, but I do not suppose it would do much good. I cannot live other people's lives for them, and it would be arrogant of me to expect that every time I open my mouth and pronounce something that I am going to be listened to with awed reverence. Life just does not work that way.

Love Dreams

If you dream that you have problems with your sight then you certainly are being fooled in a relationship – watch out for lies and infidelities! A dream of strong and lovely perfume heralds the entry of a very passionate lover into your life. Interpreting your dreams can be a lot of fun and you will be surprised by the accuracy of some of the things you will be able to predict about your love life. There are all sorts of things appearing in dreams to indicate good and bad forecasts of love. Broken knives, broken rings, blindness, and an empty hearth, all indicate, as you will probably suspect, difficulties and failure in love. But flowers, perfume, milk, pleasant colours and sensations are all very favourable omens. If you dream of fire, cool your temper or expect major rows in your relationship. Many people dream of flying – that, according to certain psychologists, is a straightforward omen of needing - and of probably getting – a very healthy phase in your sex life.

Love Spells

From time to time, as I have already stated, people confuse psychic ability with witchcraft and they ask me for a love spell. I have to admit that the notion of spells fascinates me, although the whole idea of invoking supernatural powers to alter the course of natural events repulses me. There is no magic more potent than natural chemistry between two people. My own feeling about spells is that they work because the intention of the user is so powerful that they throw out an irresistible vibration that attracts the other party to them.

A close woman friend deeply in love with her man and feeling that his attention was straying asked me for a love spell. 'Are you absolutely sure? Because once this particular spell is cast, you'll have him for life.' I can still see her face set and determined. 'That's what I want.' Her name, and his, were written on a piece of paper and a circle was drawn around the names. Then she folded up the paper and sealed it with a tiny speck of blood from her ring finger. Holding the paper she chanted I will bid, I will bind, I will hold thee to my mind.'

His attention to her after that became so possessive and claustrophobic that she could not handle the relationship and wanted to end it. She moved out of Ireland, kept her new job and new address a secret from him (all her friends were sworn to secrecy), went ex-directory with her telephone number, but he still managed to track her down, swearing his undying love and devotion. Eventually she married a very strong man who had to deal with the previous boyfriend who by then had turned into a certifiable pest.

If you make a spell - and I truly do *not* advocate it – be prepared to take full responsibility for what you are doing and what the consequences might be. A more pleasant and more harmless spell is to take an apple, cut it in two and push a clove into either half. The cloves represent you and the partner you wish to win. Then tie up the apple with red twine or ribbon and bury it under an oak tree. You should get your partner shortly after that. I have heard from several people that it really *does* work I am not sure if that one works so effectively – because it is a genuine spell or because the person being spelled for cannot resist the glint in the eye of the spellmaker!

Lisdoonvarna

In September there is a matchmaking festival in Lisdoonvarna in the West of Ireland. Men and women of all types go there, some just for fun, others in the hope of finding a partner. Brides-to-be come from as far away as America looking for a husband. Some have a romantic notion of the Irish farmer – a lot of farmers trot off to Lisdoonvarna to show themselves to the female world which believes them to be good, solid men with a natural way of life and sound values. On the whole, this is true. They are a hard-working bunch, unpretentious, and faithful to their wives, providing well for their children and demanding little for themselves out of a life-time of service to the farm and community.

But there is a strain in the breed imbued with the belief that a firm sixty-five year old jaw and fifty acres of land makes them a catch any girl would die for. Some of these decided against an early marriage on the grounds that with their mother in the house it would be unfair (more likely unwise) to bring in a wife to the farm. It is a well-known fact that two women cannot peacefully share the same kitchen floor.

Others reacted against a hasty marriage, preferring a twenty or thirty year courtship to make sure that they thoroughly know and understand the qualities of the girl with whom they choose to enter marriage.

Preparing himself for Lisdoonvarna, a man of about sixty-four or five came to see me. A good quality waistcoat stretched across his midriff. Quality tweeds and expensive brogues spoke of money and a certain rural refinement of taste. The hands clutching the polished blackthorn stick were weathered but fairly smooth. He worked, but had help, not everything was left to him. He must also have a fair bit of farm hardware and machinery, he was certainly not worn out with manual work.

'I'm off to Lisdoonvarna to look for a wife. What are me chances? I want a natural blond not much over twenty-six. Can you give me initials?'

Whether it was confidence or arrogance, this farmer was sure that he would meet a girl, even one young enough to be his grand-daughter, all he needed was the initials. Often I am asked for initials; meaning, can I tell a person the initials of the person they are going to marry. Some clairvoyants can do this, I cannot, anymore than I can read my own cards. It is not a gift I have, or am ever likely to have.

Chapter Five

Money

'**C**an you tell me if I am going to win the National Lottery?' has to be the most frequently asked question of either me, or any other clairvoyant. When the National Lottery was first started a few years ago I used to get really excited when I saw a combination of cards showing that someone I was doing a reading for was going to win. There is a distinct pattern of cards to show winning money. But I have since had a complete reverse of feeling. *Anyone* for whom I predicted a big win got it eventually, but *all* returned at some stage to tell me their subsequent experiences. Their circumstances were all quite different but their feelings about the win were the same and are best summed up by a Dublin woman married with children whose husband started drinking after their big lottery win.

'I'd give anything, to go back to the days before we won. We were happier, then, than we knew. He drinks all the time and I feel I've lost a husband and the children a good father. He divided the money up and gave the family, his and mine, a share.' Her voice was weary, as though tired of reciting this. 'But they quarrelled with us, well, me really, he was never around much. They grudged us winning, as though we'd no real right to it. I was reminded by this person and that of favours done in the past as though there were some sort of account book kept over the years that now we had to pay back.' She turned expensive rings on her fingers. Her hands despite her life of ease now were still work roughened, 'It's as though we've all become enemies. I chose a lovely mountain bike for his nephew, but he looked at it as if it was dirt and said I could afford better. And that from a child of twelve.' For a moment her voice was animated indignation.

'I think I'd like a separation from him, get back to a life I know. But you can't put the clock back, can you? I'll get the separation anyway, be a bit independent of them all. After all, I can afford it can't I?'

I was sad for her because I remembered a time when she first came to me for a reading and had been so proud and happy that she and her family were going on their first family holiday since she and her husband got married. They went to a caravan in Tramore and it rained but they had a wonderful time, she told me.

There were many other similar emotional experiences, although some people had managed to put their winnings to very good economic use.

What I say to people now is, 'Put the money away' into an account for twenty-eight days and do not touch it. At the end of that time you will know the strengths and weaknesses of everyone around you.'

Money can be forecast also by the set of lines in a palm that indicate if there is wealth ahead. There is a network of lines beneath the index finger, and a criss-cross of lines on the base section of the index finger. The presence of these lines guarantees great financial security, and, at some stage a big increase in income. Some people have other lines in their hands showing that they will not hold onto money or that they will give it away to their families, but I believe that each person has the right to spend their money as they choose.

Good Luck and Bad Luck in Money

I am not a great believer in luck, I think you make your own. We all choose careers, partners, and patterns of expenditure. We exercise choice. But some people do seem to acquire money more easily than others. People who regularly win competitions appear to be lucky. They are not. What they practice is the art of competition. They say there is a knack to winning. They figure out, in slogan competitions for instance, what it is that the competition organisers are looking for, and they deliver. Also they actually *enter*. 'I wouldn't win an argument,' certain people often say in their own defence. Of course they would not win because, by and large they do not enter anything. People who regularly win study competitions, enter just about everything and anything going, and keep on trying. They acquire an attitude of mind that they are entitled to win and they do.

The gambler, whether on sports events or with stocks and shares (respectably called an investor), who is successful, is, I believe, psychic. They get a gut feeling about certain companies or horses and they also rely on that same instinct to tell them when to sell shares. They also acquire a very sound body of knowledge about their chosen field of speculation.

Other people may call them lucky but they only appear so. They are not protected by some mysterious occult agency, they are guided by knowledge and recognition of their own psychic ability.

One businessman I know claims to have been dogged by bad luck in business over the past few years.

'It feels as though something dark and unlucky dogs my every footstep and I just can't do a thing right.'

What actually happened is that he made a series of ill-advised buys, did not allow himself enough working capital, had to borrow from the bank, and had not carried out a feasibility study prior to trading in order to establish whether or not there would be any demand for the goods he supplied. In other words, he broke just about every rule in the business book. It was not bad luck it was stupidity.

Generally people who win, expect to win. If you want to win at something expect it as of right, then it will happen. Some people call it positive thinking, I call it common sense.

Money Omens

You *can* gauge when it is right to have a small gamble. If pigeons feature in your dreams, your garden, or even more potent, one comes into your house you are obviously giving out a strong psychic vibration that money is coming your way. People know their own future subconsciously. Their subconscious tells them when money is coming, they radiate financial confidence and simply wait for good financial news. Birds are messengers between the worlds, they sense things about people, pick up on the vibrations that human beings throw out.

My own theory about the presence of pigeons – even if it is only pigeon droppings – close to someone about to come into a lot of money is based on bygone days and poverty. Pigeons were a great pot-filler for country people. If a poor person went stalking abroad the pigeon sensed he might end up in their pot and flew away. Whereas feathered Freddie had nothing to fear from a wealthy person or one about to become wealthy. All right you can punch holes in that one if you like but I like it as a theory.

Finding a four-leaf clover was always said to be a sure sign of money coming and some people believe that money will come to them if they carry a particular money charm. My favourite money omen is one that never ever fails. If my left palm itches then I know that money is on the way. I may not be consciously aware at the time of the possible source of the money but it never fails to arrive. I probably subconsciously pick up that someone who owes me money is about to pay me or give me a gift (a rare event). My subconscious mind sends a signal to my left palm and I can plan a little spending spree.

Money Dreams

Having a dream that you are counting or finding money is not necessarily a sign that money is on its way, any more than a dream about being poor, or just plain anxious about money, is a sign of approaching poverty. The most powerful dream signifying money is on the way, or that you need have no more worries about money, is a rather disgusting one – Any dream about excrement is a dream about money whether it is your own someone else's, an animals, or whatever. And, the greater the quantities in the dream, the more of a mess you were in, or were conscious of, the more money is coming to you. Another curious dream signifying approaching money is that of hair growing on some unusual part of the body. Again the more abundant the hair in this case, the greater the sum of money.

Thinking – Money and Security

I accept that often when a person tells me that they want money what they really mean is that they want freedom from anxiety about being able to pay bills, or, they may wish that they can provide sufficient to send their children to college. They want enough to make them happy, to give them what they currently desire. There is nothing worse than to suffer the torment of never having quite enough even for modest needs. But some people think in poverty terms all the time.

One very wealthy woman (by *anyone's* standards) in the Bahamas asked me to look at her palm lines to see if she was coming into money. Her hand showed an abundance of money and material possessions, yet she felt anxious about money, afraid it would never be enough, or that she might suffer loss in the future. She was a Taurean. Although I do not accept as gospel what astrologers have to say about personality, or the future events as predicted by them, I have noticed that it is a Taurean trait to be constantly worried about money and future security. I have come to accept, therefore, that certain personalities *think* in poverty terms, and as a result, will always, by their own relative thinking, be poor.

Other people have a capacity to enjoy life, spending what they can get their hands on, and rarely troubling to think about future security, or provide for it. Of the two types, I prefer the latter, they are much easier to be with. What the Taurean type is doing wrong is not thinking money, but thinking poverty, and that is what they get. They rarely win anything. What they have has usually been acquired through hard work. In contrast, Pisceans often appear flighty, particularly over monetary affairs, but they are usually very hardworking and shrewd where money is concerned. They have strong psychic feelings about money and business, and, without being able to provide a rationale for apparently intuitive actions, seem to hit on exactly the right moment to look for a new job, buy a National Lottery ticket, or start a new business.

Finding lost Money

He shone from the top of his bald head to the tips of his polished boots. He wore a neat, well-cut navy suit, and under his arm he carried a rolled copy of the London Times. I watched him carefully as he walked towards my desk, something did not seem quite right, and I could not pin-point what it was. He had the appearance of a successful businessman; there was an aura of money around him (a lot of money) yet, he was not what he first appeared to be.

I looked at his hands, strong square working hands, scrupulously clean. Smooth skin, very slightly weathered. I judged him to be about sixty years of age. He had a big nose, denoting a strong personality. Then I noticed his eyes, light and clear grey and saw with surprise that he was subjecting me to the same careful scrutiny I gave him. He took the measure of me for, perhaps, a couple of minutes, then he slapped the newspaper down on the table.

'I'll be honest I can't read that. He had a sharp Dublin accent.

Taking the seat opposite me, he sat very upright with his hands clasped in his lap.

'I can't read or write and I carry that around to make people think I can. But I wouldn't want to fool you because I'm here on an honest errand.'

I sensed a proud but reticent man, one who would confide in very few with a need to unburden himself of some trouble.

'I've made a fair bit of money, I'm careful with it but I'll spend if I have to. I've had money stolen from me. I want to know who took it.'

I offered him the cards which he shuffled and handed back to me. After laying them out in three's I studied them, intently aware that something strange was happening. I could feel the psychic heat and energy rising in me, my palms began to heat, my fingertips felt very sensitive. Turning his palm over I looked at his palm lines and touched his line of head. He stayed still, passive, but I felt a tremendous explosion of psychic energy. It was like an electric shock through my body and into my brain where pictures began to form. I scarcely had to look at the cards or touch his palm, the pictures were crystal clear in my head as though I was watching a black and white film. This man had well developed psychic powers which he used all the time, whether consciously or unconsciously I could not tell.

'I can see a yard, a breakers yard, there are cars, hundreds of them all piled up on each other. You own the place, you have done for years. Before that you travelled with your family throughout Ireland, but I think you were born in England. You settled in that yard in Dublin and you have made a lot of money. You always carry a large sum of money in your pocket, one or two thousand pounds at least.

'You love a woman with slim features and dark hair, she carried flowers a lot. Roses.'

I could see masses of red roses, I could even smell them. It was a vivid and powerful image. Her face was lovely with the kind gentle eyes of a young girl, even though she looked to be about fifty years of age. The pictures rolled on, the scene changed to a small office. It must have been up steps because I could see through a window down into the breakers yard below.

The woman's son works for you. You like him, he is like a son to you.'

I sensed the man opposite me change, I looked at him; his face seemed exactly the same. But there was a slight increase in the psychic energy he sent out. It made me work harder to gain control of my own psychic power. Psychic power running amok not only interferes with electrical apparatus, it also leaves me physically drained to the point of extreme fatigue, which sometimes takes days from which to recover.

The pictures in my mind rolled on, but now became so vivid that it was as though the walls of the room became a projection screen.

I saw a young man, lighter in colouring, but with the woman's features enter the office. He looked around, furtively, then went to the jacket hanging on the back of the door put his hand into the inside pocket, pulled out a roll of notes stuffed them inside his coat and left.

As he left the office, there was a sound outside the window. This time I had the extraordinary experience of feeling that I had moved into the scene. On going to the window I saw my enquirer in fierce argument with a red-haired young man with angry eyes. The sounds faded and I was aware of having moved backwards, around a desk filled with ordered piles of papers, to the back of the office. I could actually feel a wooden wall at my back and smell the woody, dusty atmosphere of the small place.

The door opened, my enquirer entered. I held my breath, feeling it was bizarre that he seemed not to see me. He went to the window, looked out for a moment, shrugged, then went to the back of the door for his jacket. As he put it on, his hand went as by instinct to his inside pocket. Realising that his money had been taken seemed to make him immensely sad rather than angry.

He stayed quite still for what seemed to me, an invisible watcher, a very long time. I could feel his unspoken thoughts.

'You will be unhappy to know that the boy you trusted, your lover's son stole your money,' I heard myself relate aloud.

Across the desk from me, my enquirer smiled, shaking his head. 'You told me, already, that he did. You said it all, just as it was, you might have been there.'

As he spoke I was aware of weariness creeping through me, and that I must have been perspiring a lot. It came as a surprise to learn that I had been talking throughout, as I watched, because I was not aware of that. In a way, that bit frightened me more than anything else, because that was the first time my clairvoyant ability had entirely taken me over. This man must have the most extraordinary powers, I thought, because he caused that to happen.

'You don't seem to mind', I commented.

'The lad you saw me fighting with is my nephew, my brother's boy. He thinks I'm going against my own kind to have my woman's boy running things. But he can read and write and I can't. My nephew wanted me to put him out.' 'I suppose you will now that you know he's a thief.'

'I will not. I have his measure, I had it anyway. But I can bear the thing. What I could not have borne was the shame of knowing that it was my own kind and kin who robbed me. That would have been much worse.'

Picking up his paper, tucking it under his arm, straightening his tie, he went off looking like a bank manager about to give some wretched customer a reprieve.

After he had gone I felt as though a huge charge of energy had been taken from the room. Normality was returning, bringing with it a headache and the customary fatigue. I felt real disappointment as there was so much I would have liked to ask that man about himself and his extraordinary power. His cards were still laid out on the desk, I looked at them but could make no sense of them at all. It was as if, when he left, he drew some psychic veil over himself and his affairs.

Wills and Ways

Money can do a lot, but it also tends to bring out the very worst side of human nature. Money earned and well spent can bring a great sense of satisfaction, pride even. But money up for grabs like prize money, or inherited money does unpleasant things to people. Some of the most difficult readings I have had to do have been concerned with people feeling cheated over a will.

A very pleasant middle-aged couple came to me after the death of the woman's mother, on whose farm the couple had lived since marrying. The husband had taken over the duties of the farm as his wife's brothers were all away working in America. Being the only daughter, she was expected by the family, and by society in West Cork to look after her mother. This she had done, she told me, and I believed her. Her hands were kind and gentle, her manner very submissive and enduring. Her husband was the sort to trust other people, take them at their word, and work accordingly. His wife's mother had promised them the farm and he did not grudge the twenty-six years spent working it.

He did not grudge it until his mother-in-law died and they found that the farm had been left to the eldest son, a chemist, working in America. The farm had been the mother's left to her by her parents, and hers to dispose of as she wished. The son in America did not want the place and proposed selling it. The couple could buy if they chose, but had not the money. When farmers tell you they have no money you usually have to suspend belief for a while, it's a well worn story, but in this case I believed them. They would not have come to me otherwise, they would simply have paid up. As it turned out, between their own savings, and loans from their children and his brother and sister, they did buy the farm. But it is a fact that sometimes when a person says one thing about their intentions for a will they might do something quite different.

Farmers

With the above story in mind I was quite firm in my advice to a young man who came to me wondering if he should work the family farm for his mother (his sisters were married and living in England, were very comfortably off, and had said that they were quite willing to give up any claim on the farm), or get her to sell up and move into the town from which she had originally come.

To move might have seemed like the best solution because he already worked in the town as a teacher (a job he did not much like). A possessive love of land is very strong in Irish people and the young teacher confessed a real hankering to farm as his father had done before him. He had worked hard academically to please his mother and had gone into teaching at her instigation, she had been a teacher until her retirement.

Knowing that people change their minds about a will, with experience behind me, and understanding perfectly well that whatever his sisters might say far distant in England comfortably off, that when their mother died the Irish hunger for land might take over and they might look for their share.

If you are to have the incentive to take over the farm you *must* get everything in writing, get it signed over to you.

The cards show this to be the soundest advice. 'Get a legal document from your sisters acknowledging that they give up their claim on the property. According to you the farm even well managed, can only support one family.'

About four years later a big healthy-looking girl came to me for a reading.

'I love my husband, and want our marriage to work, but I just cannot stand his mother. She lives with us on the farm, it was signed over to my husband when we were both teaching at the same school. He gave up his job to run it but his mother never stopped interfering. I thought we could all get on well together, I'm not a difficult person to live with.'

I could believe that she looked intelligent and adaptable.

'We have our own part of the house to live in, it's supposed to be private, but she just walks in whenever she pleases without a bye-your leave. She even comes into our bedroom. If I say anything at all, she reminds me that I married in and have no rights at all.' The girl flushed. 'I still teach and my husband is very glad of my money, the farm is not doing well at the moment.'

Her cards showed that she was right the economic situation would improve after the next harvest, and the dairy herd were improving in yield the time. Within the cards also there was a ten of spades next to the ace of hearts and ace of diamonds. This girl wanted a son and had not produced one.

'And there's no medical reason why not, we're both healthy. My mother-in-law never stops giving out about it. She talks about it to other people in front of me saying I'm too selfish and fond of myself to have a child.' She stopped and stayed silent for a few minutes and I could sense from reading her palms her deep misery, hurt and a growing resentment. Unfortunately the cards showed the mother-in-law would not change her jealous, possessive attitude to her son or her resentment towards the daughter-in-law. The poor girl was stuck in a miserable no-win situation because the man she married had no willpower at all, and did not in the least mind his mother's possessive attitude which he thought was normal love.

A couple of years later I read in the paper that the young man had been killed in a tractor accident on his farm. He was mourned the article said, by his wife and mother and two sisters in England. It made no mention of children of the dead man. I thought of those two women cloistered in hatred on the farm. The wife luckily had sole ownership of it now and she was still young enough to remarry and have children – what an interesting situation would develop if she married again. With a farm and a pensionable job she made a very good catch and might get a husband strong enough to deal with the vindictive old mother-in-law.

I subsequently stopped applying the experience of one person to another and left my judgements solely to what the palms, cards and my psychic ability told me was appropriate.

Chapter Six

Health

There are several natural means of checking on good and bad health. Dreams, palms and the palm lines, the cards, psychosomatic evidence of mental stress. I shall review these in this chapter and include a little on hypnosis, regression, faith-healing and crystal magic, as these last four are related to health but are most frequently, and quite wrongly, associated with clairvoyance.

The request, 'Don't tell me anything bad,' is often followed up by 'How long am I going to live?'. A reading beginning with that structure obviously invites me to reply, 'A hundred and fifty years, at least.'

Once, at the Dandelion Market, on St Stephen's Green, in Dublin I watched a Chinese man, a psychic, at work. He had a long table, elaborately laid out, at which he stood inviting people to have their futures read by him. A young man approached the table and engaged in conversation with the psychic. He looked at the various papers, dishes and candles, laid out on the bright cloth and with a slightly embarrassed shrug – it was a very big, populated and public market – he sat down behind the table, facing what began to be an audience.

The Chinese man began a series of small flourishes, rather like an old-fashioned fair-ground dentist about to pull a tooth. He noted things about the young man's date of birth, consulted a chart, looked at his hands, and then placed both hands on what seemed now, more of a patient's than a client's head.

'You are going to die at the age of fifty-two.'

I have never forgotten the fearful gasp that went up, our own instinctive revulsion. Still in my mind I can see the young man pale and get up from his seat looking unhappy and confused. The Chinese man looked completely baffled as his audience backed away. His face said, 'But what did I do wrong?'

Our attitude to death is cultural. In the West we do not discuss it. If the suggestion is made to a person that they should make a will it is considered morbid, or bad luck, or at worst, that the person making the suggestion is plotting, hoping for, or anticipating, the other death.

In other cultures death is seen as a natural end to life, it is discussed, anticipated, and sometimes even welcomed.

The one thing no one needs a psychic to tell them is if they are going to die. The only two sure things in life anyone can know is that they were born and that they will die. Yet, having knowledge of death and having a pre-announced date are two separate things. Maybe we should cultivate greater faith in the after-life, or somehow develop a philosophy that enables us to face death more placidly. We have phrases, such as, 'He lost his battle with cancer', to indicate that death is an enemy that has to be fought. But if we live with a philosophy that means that we feel obliged to fight against the inevitable it must, surely, diminish the quality of life. Paradoxically, while thoroughly understanding that, I can also understand the dread a person would have if I were to say, 'You'll only live another six months.'

Life Line

The life line tells me a great deal about a person's health. The length of it does not necessarily indicate the length of life. However, Agatha Christie once recalled being struck by the fact that many young men in the late Edwardian era had short life lines – palmistry was vogue – and subsequently died very young in the First World War. A short life-line indicates to me a person without much ambition for themselves, that any hopes for the future are centred on someone else. My interpretation also includes a belief that a person with a short life line has a poor self-image and a lack of confidence.

I have seen palm lines change, growing longer, deepening. If a person is ill then the life line is faded. A very pale, almost non-existent line shows a person who is very ill. But people recover and when they do the life line is clear, with a pinkish colour and a deeper groove.

One plump, clear-skinned young woman wanted to know if she was to have more children. The cards showed that it was possible, but there was a doubt. Her children lines – the tiny vertical lines at the base of the small finger – showed several children, but they were faint with definite horizontal lines through the children lines indicating loss of children. With family planning and contraception it is quite difficult to say just how many children a person will have. The cards are a much better guide.

I looked at her life line – something I do not normally do when looking at fertility – to see seven tiny feathered lines grouped together at a particular point on her life line. I had learned something new – one learns all the time.

'Have you ever had a miscarriage or still-birth?'

'Three miscarriages and two still-births.'

'How many children have you now?'

'Two.'

'Are you pregnant now?'

'Definitely not.'

I was in a terrible quandary. For one thing, I was not sure of myself and what I was reading, my sense of intrigue had quietened to a feeling of responsibility to this woman.

'If I were you, I'd call it a day. Two children seems about right for you.'

'Do you mean that if I went ahead and had another pregnancy that I would miscarry, or suffer another still-birth?'

'That is my opinion. But I do get things wrong, I'm not always right.'

Her features crumpled up, she looked like a little girl.

'I don't think I could survive the agony of losing another baby. No one knows how awful it is. They say things like, 'He's in a better place', or, 'Well, it was only twelve weeks, it didn't count', they mean well I know that, but no one understands.'

I learned something else that day, too and it humbled me because those were exactly the sort of stupid things I had said until then without any idea of how hurtful they were. I could read in other lines on her palm the type of reaction she would have to the news.

Her head line was deep and straight, she was logical, clear thinking, not given to hysteria, or even depression. She would weigh what I said and make her own decisions about her future fertility patterns.

Head Line

The head line shows a great deal about a person's mental health or ill-health. A straight line, as I have already stated, is logical, practical, showing a person who will eat, drink, and live fairly moderately. When confronted with a problem it will be sorted out with the minimum of fuss.

A head line curving down slightly often belongs to the creative thinker, a person drawn to the unusual. In mental health terms it also indicates someone inclined to headaches, down moods and a vivid imagination. This type who, if a bad headache persisted, thinks it a brain tumour.

When the head line slopes down to the opposite side of the palm it shows a person given to dramatics, big mood swings, hysteria and often, real and deep depression. This does *not* mean that this is inevitable, but it does mean that a person with this sort of palm should be aware of what is inherent in their character and make up and try not to over react to events.

Only the other day a girl with just this sort of head line told me:

'I thought I was depressed, really depressed a lot. I kept bursting into tears (her marriage had broken down) and felt that everything was awful. Then I started writing down when these moods came on and realised that they only lasted twenty minutes, they didn't dominate my day at all. Thinking about them did, though. After that I felt a lot better.'

What she did was, to take control of her moods and pre-disposition to depression, and for her it worked.

Hand Shape

The overall shape of the hand is a good indicator as to future health patterns. A long narrow hand belongs to someone who will always worry a lot, will agonise over decisions and have crisis of conscience. The square hand is full of energy, cannot sit still for long, and to be happy and healthy, needs a great deal of activity and many projects to run. Without activity this sort of person is moody, unhappy and begins to fancy that illness is all around.

Where there is a rounded, fleshy shape on the side of the palm opposite the thumb this shows a person very fond of food and sex. To the slender palmed person this type seems gross, self-indulgent and a walking health menace. In my own experience, they are healthy, long living and often look a good deal younger than their years.

Although I have great respect for vegetarians, particularly those who abstain on the grounds of conscience, and I adore vegetables without being a vegetarian, they do not seem to enjoy as good physical or mental health as meat eaters.

The positive side of vegetarianism is that it has brought vegetables to the centre of the table, promoted them to the position they should always have as part of a healthy diet. You can look at your horoscope, into your palm, consult your dreams, but it does not make a bit of difference, your health depends on what you eat and what sort of environment you live in. If those two things are not in place, then the other positive factors are merely pale compensations. Many vegetarians lack energy, are pre-occupied with their physical health (and everyone else's) and carry an overly heavy burden of responsibility for the environment. We *all* care. There is a type of man often seen trudging the pavements in London. He wears a jumper he probably knitted himself, his silky hair frames a sallow, gaunt face, while his haunted eyes rake the crowds inviting them to notice the infant strapped papoose style to his back. Notice me, his vibrations howl. Notice was a good FATHER I am. Whatever you do, never, ever, engage in conversation with such a man because he will begin gently to inform you of the joys of vegetarianism and end with an angry tirade against YOU. Because YOU with your filthy cigarette and the beef burger you ate last Tuesday are all responsible for the existence of Sellafield, or Windscale as it was formerly called, (it will probably be called Rosegarden next).

What has done far more for vegetarianism than the morally correct and rather judgmental vegetarian environmentalist is the influx of absolutely delicious Chinese, Indian and Middle Eastern food. These are all more or less vegetarian, meat is not essential to most of those dishes, they are cheap to buy, most easy to prepare, and heaven to eat.

Dreams of Sickness

To dream of actually being sick, vomiting, is a sign of approaching money. Dreaming of eating and enjoying food often indicates good health. But any dream of the throat or neck is a sign that the dreamer needs a medical check-up – fast!

Pain in the neck

There is a school of thought, to which I am increasingly drawn, that evidence of bodily affliction is an indicator of something wrong in the person's life. Often when doing a reading, I get a sensation of back pain.

"Do you suffer from backache?' I asked one middle-aged farmer. 'I do. I've had it for the past five years and nothing I do seems to shift it. I went to the bone-setter three or four times, but it always comes back.'

His palms and cards showed that he had been through five or six years of difficulty in his marriage, had quarrelled with his eldest son who had left home, and his farming was difficult. To add to all of that he had borrowed money he was not able to repay easily.

I suspected that when his difficulties cleared up, as the cards showed they would, his backache would go away.

A woman who came regularly for readings enjoyed radiant health, had a lovely husband, beautiful children, and a successful career which she managed with ease. All comparison is odious as it only leads to dissatisfaction and envy, but I have to confess to feeling a bit of envy of her.

'I know how lucky I am and I thank God for it.' She would often say. I liked her the more for it because I knew she meant it. She came for readings purely for fun.

So, when she came to me with a pain in her neck I took it very seriously, she had never had a day's illness in her life, and was practically sprouting good health. After only a few minutes of the reading, she burst out:

'Can you tell me when my sister-in-law will get her house? Is there anything in the cards about a house contract?'

I knew her sister-in-law, and respected her ability in her job, she was, and is, a very good accountant. But she is also a judgmental little ferret who thinks all mothers should give up careers and stay at home to mind the children. In this particular instance just talking about it was a help.

What I do not like about the psychosomatic theory is that it makes a person responsible for their own health, and that must be terribly hard on some poor soul told that they have cancer and have not long to live.

Faith Healers

Clairvoyants and faith healers have long been associated together, although, in my view, there is absolutely no link whatsoever. People do not have to be believers for the cards to show the truth. Many people do claim to have been cured by a visit to a faith healer, or cured by a miracle after visiting a holy shrine of pilgrimage. All I can say is, if it makes you feel better, if you feel greater confidence after such a visit, go right ahead. It is a harmless enough occupation.

Hypnosis

For centuries hypnosis and clairvoyance were as practically one and the same. Psychics, particularly as seen on film, in books, or written about years ago, were always alleged to go into the light trance-like state we now call hypnosis. The psychic, or clairvoyant, has extra sensory perception, can read the future, the past and look at what is going on in an enquirer's life at the present moment. As a psychic I know perfectly well that it is random. I do not know what aspect of a person's life will surface during a card reading. Sometimes people say, 'Can you tell me anything about the past?. What they really mean is, 'I would like some sort of proof that what you've told me about the future is correct, and the way I'll know that is if you are accurate about the past.'

Occasionally a reading deals almost exclusively with the past. The reason for that being, that there exists in a person's current life some sort of blockage, some inability to go forward, make decisions, to form good relationships, because of events, perhaps in childhood that have remained unresolved. A reading can be enormously beneficial then.

What the cards show is what is important to a person *now*. A very nice young girl in New York asked me to read her cards as she was very, very anxious about the future. I saw all sorts of nice things, including, by purest coincidence, a dark and very handsome man she was likely to marry. She said she did have a dark boyfriend and was planning to marry him. She thanked me politely for her reading and re-joined guests at the party we both enjoyed.

A while later another guest came up to me and asked me if I was able to be of any help to the girl.

'She's in real trouble. Her parents are divorced, her dad is a real nice guy but he's dying of cancer. Her mother is a regular witch and she's nagging the girl to get all she can out of her old man before he dies.'

I was appalled. Nothing of this had shown in her cards. Nothing at all, and I had picked up nothing like that from her hand. It is no harm to be wrong sometimes, it stops me being too sure of myself. But I was very sorry in that instance.

She would have benefited far more from a visit to a good, *properly qualified* hypnotherapist. There are many people who get a book from the library, read it, and claim to be a hypnotherapists. Anyone considering going to a hypno-therapist should ask to see their qualifications before making an appointment. Hypnotherapy suggests to the client that they will become deeply relaxed, in that state they are more able to view the past without the painful emotions that such an exercise might normally produce. If you want to become more assertive, lose weight, stop smoking, then hypnosis is a tremendous help in that. It also enables a person to discuss confidentially deeply rooted fears, phobias even.

Some hypnotherapists make many claims about the healing power of hypnosis. I am not sure that hypnosis can heal, unless it is one of the ailments induced by stress and anxiety, but it can certainly manage pain much better. No decent hypnotist or hypnotherapist would have a client reduced to a zombie-like state, or gyrating like a clown to entertain people, that would be pointless and silly. Neither would a good hypnotist try to gain control of another person's mind. That is a very good theme for a film or book, but in real life it does not actually work. Not unless the person was credulous to the point of imbecility, in that case anyone could control the mind.

Regression to Past Life

There is a theory that we have had many previous lives and that when we pass from this one some souls wait in the astral planes between this world and the next, and come back to a different existence.

A hypnotherapist I know and trust told me of a very difficult woman patient of his; she was quite unable to consummate her marriage. Her vagina spasmed whenever her husband and she tried to have intercourse. They loved each other very much. They went to the hypnotherapist as a last resort, thinking, maybe, that there was something in childhood so dreadful, abuse perhaps, that it had been buried deeply in her subconscious.

After several therapy sessions nothing more frightening or awful had come out other than one of her brothers once called her 'skinny'. It amused her if anything. So, the hypnotherapist regressed her to a previous life to see if anything surfaced there that might explain her distressing condition.

In a deeply relaxed state she went back to a life in London. She was a young Welsh girl, from a deeply religious family, who had gone to London to serve as a maid in a big house. There the master of the house had brutally raped her. Her subsequent pregnancy had caused her banishment from the house. She could not go home to Wales where her religious family would certainly not have received her. She found her solution in the river Thames.

After this revelation the transformation was extraordinary. Her sex life gradually began to happen, naturally and gently. But much later she did confide to the hypnotherapist that, she had occasional flitting 'memories' of something dreadful happening to her body and had been terribly afraid that someone she knew and trusted had abused her. That realisation, as well as the revelations of regression, began her healing.

Crystal Magic

Many, many people have great faith in the power of certain crystals to heal them, to draw good influences to them, or to fend off evil influences. I use a crystal, as I have already stated, when searching for missing people or animals and find it very effective. But in matters of health, common sense, an appeal to the expert (doctor or consultant) is to me a natural first step. Good diet, healthy eating and sound sleep are all the practical, logical steps to good health.

A reader wrote into my psychic column in the magazine asking if she would be protected from AIDS in unsafe sex if she wore a crystal around her neck. There's one born every minute, isn't there?

Chapter Seven

Work

The biggest influence in anyone's life is their work. If the person has no paid occupation outside the home, it is an even bigger influence. The work a person does defines their status. If a woman admits to being, 'only a housewife', society dismisses her entirely. Her claim to fame and status is won by entering the competition Housewife of the Year. I have never been sure if that competition is a joke or a punishment.

One does not admit to being a doctor, one proclaims it, and the rewards in terms of social approval and status are enormous. Occupation shapes our social attitudes; what kind of newspaper we buy, how we decorate our homes, how much is earned. Education is valued. A child's future chances in education, occupation, earning ability, the kind of future marriage partner, leisure pursuits, just about every aspect of future life, are all governed by parental occupation.

Even health patterns are ruled by the occupation of the individual. It is often said that you never see a bald traveller. Maybe not, but you do not often see an elderly one either. I grew up on the maxim that hard work is good for the body. Compare the man who owns the land – and plenty of it – to the man who merely labours on it. One is healthy, good-looking and fit for his age, the other, of similar age, appears much older.

Depression, and even suicide rates, are high amongst farmers, but for those who love the work and the land it is a real joy. They feel an immense pride in themselves and have the ability to endure through hardship and prosperity. Many farmers, not necessarily those who are wealthy and successful, have an individuality and sense of self-worth that sustains them and makes them the attractive people that prospective spouses go to Lisdoonvarna looking for. It is the self-worth, or lack of it, conferred by the job done that is the most affective on personality.

I lectured at third level for fifteen years and saw over and over again students who should never have been in college – they were there because parents pushed them into courses they either were not able for, or interested in. When they failed, as some did, they carried the stigma of failure for years to come.

If you give to life what you can and take from it what you need, you will not go too far wrong.

The occupation a person chooses should be one that suits the skills and personality of the individual, otherwise the individual can never be happy. The pursuit of happiness is the most worthwhile goal a person can aim for. I noticed that lots of young people who had emigrated from Ireland to work in either England or America had this aim in mind. I used to think that if they would work as hard at home, and be prepared to roll up their sleeves, and do any job the way they would abroad, then they could be well off and happy. Thinking it over of course that is not true. The bank manager would cringe to see his son working as a garage mechanic. It is a silly attitude in my opinion but it is also a social reality and will probably take a very long time to change.

It ought to be the case that a person with a boring, low-status, or repetitive job, should be able to find compensation in really exciting leisure activities. That is not so. A boring job tends to equal boring leisure. Whereas a person with a stimulating and exciting, or demanding job has the same expectations of their leisure time. The television presenter, or producer wants the same buzz and excitement out of their spare time as they have in work.

Career guidance at the age of sixteen ought to include a detailed study of the young person's horoscope, their palms, their cards, and maybe an analysis of their dreams. Stick someone into a job they dislike, are bored with, or just plain cannot do, and they only half live. Years of greyness stretch ahead and nothing ever really compensates.

People who love their work would almost do it for a hobby. They never grudge the number of hours they have to put in, or the fact that they might do something and not get paid for it. I believe that there is something out there for everyone to do, whether it is a person starting out in life, a housewife of forty-five who has never worked outside the home and is not trained for anything, a man of fifty made redundant from his job in a printers shop, or an accountant of thirty-five who wants a career change. This is where the cards and palms are really a trojan help.

The cards show whether or not a person will get promoted in their work, whether the exam they have taken will be passed, or if the firm they are working for will keep going or close down – a question of vital importance to many workers today.

Working Hands

The round hand, which is fleshy and firm to touch, often gives out heat, belongs to the powerhouse of energy, the sort of person who is always busy doing something. A gorgeous little woman has been coming to me for years for readings – she comes for a laugh, always with a group of friends, who are rather like a tribe in tow. She never stops talking, or they laughing, in her effervescent company. Her husband is a silent hardworking man who adores her and they have children. She never had much education (this type of hand is often highly intelligent and belongs to the magnate). She also has the flat, wide nails of the good organiser and open thinker.

Many committees in her parish are managed by her, and managed well and with humour. In addition to that she minds children in her home, partly to make some money and partly because she is good at it. The children she minds love her, feeling the strength of her encompassing love and energy. At Christmas time she bakes not one Christmas cake, but ten or eleven to distribute to the working mothers of the children she minds and others without the time to bake. (As a quite pointless aside, why do people still keep making Christmas cakes? Has it not occurred to those industrious little bakers yet that Christmas cake is an affliction that we could all be spared with just a little thought?)

One of this lively little woman's readings showed the seven and eight of clubs together in her cards. This means an interview – sometimes it can mean a medical consultation, but there were no supporting cards to substantiate this. I was puzzled. Knowing that she was an intelligent and able organiser was one thing, but prospective employers, as most people know, look for paper qualifications or loads of experience. Unfortunately, work in the home is never recognised as *real* work.

'The factory want someone to run their canteen. I've applied for the job. I wrote a great letter of application. I told them that even though I looked like Sharon Stone I cooked like the Galloping Gourmet, and it would be a great pity not to interview me.'

She is five foot tall and nearly as wide with red cheeks, frayed curly hair, the brightest of brown eyes and the warmest of smiles I have ever seen. But she is quite unlike the tall, shapely blond actress beauty she alleged to resemble.

Then she leaned forward, looking very shrewd, but still smiling. 'Wouldn't they interview me out of curiosity alone? And, once I'm there I'll soon convince them I'm the woman for the job.'

She not only convinced them that she was the woman for the job, she convinced them to lease her the kitchen and canteen and allow her to run it as her own business venture. In financial terms it is not a huge success, but she makes a good living and has the greatest work satisfaction imaginable.

The other type of hand, with a long slender palm, belongs to the thinker, the intellectual. Where the palm lines are many and have a criss-cross or feathered appearance then this sort of person will rise high in any work needing real brain power, but will always work better in a structured organisation as they need a boss. It is no bad sign at all, it simply means that some people are better when they have a firm set of rules and guidelines to work to, and someone in a position of responsibility to make ultimate decisions and to decide, in the event of something unusual cropping up, what should be done. Highly intelligent people do not always make good organisers or decision makers, it is not part of their make-up. When put into a managerial position, they do not function at all well.

I have often thought that banks look for over-qualified people and that the actual work many bank employees are required to do is nowhere near the level of either intelligence or qualifications of the employees. Consequently, there is dissatisfaction and boredom. For those who like banking it is marvellous career, but is suitable for a person with long narrow hands and if only the principal lines of life, head, and heart are present in the hand.

A young woman brought her son, a boy of about seventeen, for a reading. She wanted him to stay on at school, get his Leaving Certificate, and go on to college or university. Actually, she referred to university as 'uni', a term I detest, and almost always employed by those who have not been to university but want to demonstrate some sort of intimacy with it. I guessed her age to be about thirty-three or thirty-four years old. I supposed that she had become pregnant very young and married because of it. Maybe she had still been at school herself, and that she wanted her son to go to college or university was a representation of her own frustrated ambitions.

The boy had got himself an apprenticeship and wanted to qualify as an electrician. Practical commonsense would tell me that the boy should become an apprentice, get a trade behind him, and then build academically later. There are so many courses on offer now that it is quite easy to go as far, academically, as one wishes.

But he had long hands with narrow tapering fingertips, indicating extreme sensitivity, and the ability to study for the long lonely hours it takes to get a good degree and further post graduate studies. He also had a very long head line with a forked ending. That showed he would be a good academic and have a genuine love of learning. At the base of his palm there was a network of forked lines indicating a love of science and the intrigued mind that makes a good researcher. Underneath the index finger of his right hand there was a star shape of lines, showing he had the creative imagination of a writer or artist. Those lines in conjunction with the other lines in his hand and the shape of his hand and palm which had a dip in the centre of it, demonstrated to me very clearly that he had a future in research science. He would publish his work and gain, without any bother to him, a doctorate.

But he was sceptical of me, rebellious to his mother's wishes, and quite determined that he wanted to become an electrician. A fairly hostile exchange followed between mother and son.

'At least with an apprenticeship I'd be earning money. If I was dependent on you for money, I'd never hear the end of it'.

His mother looked quite appalled. She put a hand up to her mouth and shook her head. I do not know how the family resolved the matter. But I do know that while we want the young to be aware of financial reality, and to take responsibility for their own financial lives, as adults, we do sometimes go way too far and make young people feel guilty for wanting anything out of life that will cost money.

Lines of Success

There is a very interesting line starting at the base of the palm, about mid-wrist, that travels up the centre of the palm, and ends somewhere close to the base of the middle finger. It is the line of ambition and is always present in someone with a hunger for status and recognition that drives the person on to succeed in whatever career they undertake.

A rather dull woman had been coming to me for years for readings. She had always talked aimlessly about wanting to do something with her life, but never seemed to have any motivation to take even a typing course, or to get a part-time job in any capacity. Her husband was well-off, her children, uniquely, were no problem at all. She had a circle of friends with whom she played golf, went to dinner, and sometimes holidayed with. 'I could have gone to university, my parents were very keen for me to go. They were disappointed when I chose to get married at eighteen instead. So I can't complain of lack of opportunity, can I?'

Apart from wishing and moaning, I honestly could not see this woman doing any more with her life than she had already done. At forty-four years of age she was stunned when her husband very coolly announced that he was leaving her, not for another woman, but simply because she bored him. He wanted to give up his business and try a new career as a writer. There would be no financial hardship and no possibility of his changing his mind.

'I could take it if he left me for another woman, but he's leaving because I bore him.'

That realisation galvinised her into action. She decided to take up, of all things, painting. I am as familiar with the world of painting as I am with that of writing and clairvoyance. I know its taste, its texture, its every intimate demand and emotion. There was absolutely *nothing* of the painter in this woman's hand. She had no lines of imagination, had not the self-discipline to apply herself for the long, lonely hours it takes to construct a painting.

'Most artists have a very difficult time getting established and selling their work.' I ventured cautiously. 'I don't care if I never sell a damn thing. But I do want to be seen as an interesting person. I want a job that fascinates people. I've always thought of artists as off-beat, magical types. That's how I'd like people to see me.'

I will not judge her art, but I will say that she applied herself with energy, if not a bit of flair, to the whole business of becoming an artist. She set up a studio, went to some classes in Dublin to learn drawing and painting, started to exhibit, locally at first, then around the country, and gradually started selling her work.

What intrigued me was the line of success that started growing in her hand. Faint in the first few months, getting stronger and stronger over the next three years. I had not thought that lines could either fade or grow, but they do. They can and do. She is a remarkable testament to the human beings ability to take charge and control of life, and their so-called fate – to dominate, to achieve, to succeed. She makes a modest living out of her work. She still has money and property from her husband, so does not absolutely need to survive by her paint brush, and is quite well thought of by people who buy from her. Her own bonus is that she lives with a very good-looking, but much younger man, who adores her.

'My husband did me a favour when he left me and was honest enough to tell me why. It gave me the kick in the seat I badly needed. I get so much out of life now. I feel re-born.'

Religious Life

At the end of the head line there appears, a fraction of an inch away from it, a tiny grouping of lines that indicates someone who would be suitable for the religous life. Many people embrace the religous life for, what seems at the time, the right reasons. Later, they find that they are not suited, that they have physical or spiritual needs that lead them into conflict with it. A person with a fleshy hand should never enter a religious order as their sexuality will never stay disciplined to the vow of celibacy – it cannot. A person with a strong, deeply grooved headline will be too independent to obey the vow of obedience for a lifetime.

A long narrow hand, with a downward sloping headline, that feathering of fine spiritual lines, and a faint, but straight emotional line on a pale-coloured palm, all combine to make an excellent candidate for the religous vocation. Incidentally, Taureans are often very good people to embrace religous life. They have the mental capacity and toughness for work on the missions, in teaching, or amongst the sick and needy.

Running Your Own Business

A salesman in a computer firm was very upset when he came for a reading.

'I've been with the firm for years, I'm forty-seven years old. The redundancy money is good, but I'll still need to get a job. What on earth am I going to do ? I'll never get another job at my age. My experience won't count for anything at all. They're turning out youngsters with certificates, diplomas and degrees in their thousands every year. What chance do I have?'

He was right. I knew that. But he had a cross, like an X in the space between his head line and heart, or emotion, line. That shows someone who would be good at running a business venture. I have also found that when that line is present, no matter what the age, sex, or status of the person, that an opportunity to take on a business and run it as an owner or manager, will always occur in a person's life.

'Would you consider running your own business?'

He raised wry eyebrows.

'At my age? And, even if I did, all I know is the computer business. Have you any idea how much it would cost? Anyway, I'm being made redundant because there isn't enough business out there to go round. It would be like trying to open a public house for tee-totallers.'

The idea of running a public house had come from him. Somewhere in his subconscious mind was lodged the idea of becoming a publican. And, he had the cross of the self-employed man, or good manager. The side of his palm opposite the thumb was flat and straight, indicating that he liked neither food nor drink in large measure – a very good sign for a publican. Often people who go into the food or drink business, apart from those born into it, do so because they love the ambience of a public house or reataurant. When they actually have to work in the business they feel trapped and take their frustrated angry feelings out on their customers. Basil Fawlty is alive and well in many a public house, hotel, boarding house, and restaurant, all over the world.

'What about a pub? Would you consider it? You'd have your redundancy, you could borrow against your house, or even sell it.'

I expected him to reject the idea at first, he had a very straight thumb with little flexibility, indicating a person not readily receptive to new ideas. But he sat back, looking thoughtful.

'Funny you should say that. My cousin died a year ago and his wife is still running their pub. She's a lovely woman, I'm very fond of her, but she's no match for the pub business, too gentle and soft. I'd half thought of giving her a hand until I'd found a job.'

'Would she sell ?'

He shrugged. 'She might.'

The cards showed that it was entirely possible. As we talked his palm warmed, indicating that he was warming to the idea.

He did buy the public house. It would be nice to think he married the widow, too. He did not. She went off with her two children to live in London, where she is now happily married to a New Zealander. He is still a bachelor, but very happy in his thriving business. I know he is making plenty of money – I see it in the cards. But he, like other publicans, has been to the same school as many farmers, and learned to say, with conviction; 'Business isn't great. I'm pulling the devil by the tail. Just surviving.' So is his new Porsche!

Working Cards

The clubs say a lot about career and career moves. Anyone applying for a job and getting a card reading should look to see if the seven and eight of clubs appear together. That shows that an interview is coming up. It will also show the outcome of the interview. If the nine of hearts appears beside that combination then an offer will certainly be made.

An extremely able nurse came for a reading after she had put in for a post as sister in a big Bristol teaching hospital.

'I am not sure whether to go for it, or to do a course in public hygiene.'

She had drawn the seven and eight of clubs – she would be interviewed. The nine of hearts followed – she would be offered the job. But the seven and eight of spades followed immediately, showing that the job would place her under severe mental stress. She was able for the job she was in but would not be able for a promotion. The nine of clubs was turned over beside the ace of hearts. She should go on to the course she wanted to do. The nine of clubs is the card for academic success.

A prison officer I know had a reading for frivolous reasons, mainly I think, to have a gentle laugh at me. That did not bother me at all. There were some very interesting things about his character and personality in the cards, but there was also the combination of eight and nine of clubs, indicating that he would be offered a promotion.

He shook his head.

'Not possible. We know well in advance when promotions are coming up. There aren't any in the forseeable future. *And,* we know who's likely to get them.' He looked knowing. 'That's how the system works. I haven't applied for anything. If I haven't applied, I won't be considered. Simple as that.'

I know my cards, I am sure of them. The cards showed promotion. Three months after his reading he was offered a promotion, which he accepted.

Impossible? Magic? Did the card reading somehow make it all happen? Not at all. Two years earlier he had put in a routine application for promotion and when nothing happened, had forgotten all about it. His superiors had not.

Chapter Eight

Magical Places

Places I like doing readings in I call magical, happy places. My favourite place for doing a clairvoyant reading and using my psychic powers is in the small study at the back of my cottage in the countryside in County Kildare. It is quiet, peaceful and harmonious. Out of curiosity, I went recently to a hotel outside a nearby town where a psychic fair was held. The sign outside the hotel advertising the psychics was, to me, off-putting. Fair was spelt, *Fayre*, a mis-spelling I consider cheaply silly, while crystal was spelt, *crystall*. Whether that was a deliberate mis-spelling or a mistake, I am not sure, only that, for me, it created a bad first impression.

A shrewd man at the door taking the entrance fee called me love, then dearie. By now my worst fears and prejudices were forefront, so that by the time I looked at the row of mediums, palmists, card-readers, alien-spotters and sand screamers, I was well and truly jaundiced. A few people levitating and walking on fire might have added to the fair-ground atmosphere, although they were hardly needed. In such a setting I could not function at all. One part of me, as it is with all real psychics, is intensely private to the point of secrecy. One gets so used to the unwritten ruling that every reading is a private affair, each transaction between the psychic and the enquirer, alone.

Although I have attended various charity events to do readings, something I am always disposed to be co-operative about, one time the organisers of an indoor evening event asked me to do readings and asked me what I would need in the way of accommodation.

'Just a table and two chairs, and no one within earshot.'

That was promised, I was satisfied, and turned up at the appropriate time on the given day. A brisk woman with the manner and appearance of a public health nurse handed me a red scarf, gold shawl, and big ear rings. Her manner, if I did not dress up, suggested that she might give me an injection.

'I don't think they'll go with my outfit.' I was wearing a plain navy business-like suit, and navy leather shoes.

Two deep grooves appeared between her heavy eyebrows.

'We thought you'd be dressed up a bit more,' she accused.

I just refrained from saying, 'Sorry, Miss.'

'Well, come along then. We'd best get started.' Turning on her heel, she marched, head flung high, towards a stage. I trotted after her, up the steps and onto the stage to a table covered in red velvet on which gleamed a crystal ball. In another mood I might have entered into the fun of the occasion. I suppose I could have sat at that table, on stage, done some sort of party act, and entertained one and all. But I felt a sense of recoil and backed away. Despite her displeasure, we managed a compromise, and I agreed to do the readings in a tiny little room off-stage. The table and two chairs were moved into the cubby-hole, the crystal ball despatched to somewhere else, out of my sight, and I sat at the table.

As the 'nurse' went out, she looked back over her shoulder. 'No smoking.'

In retrospect I have to admit that part of my feeling of recoil had to do with the very defensive stage I was still at about my psychic ability. Every time someone either sneered at it, or just asked me a lot of interested questions I always had a very protective reaction. Nowadays I just accept that there will always be people – perfectly sane and rational – with the right to be hostile, critical, or overly-credulous, so that they regard the whole business as the practice of the magic arts, and myself as some sort of keeper of miraculous properties.

One Monday morning in winter I went to early Mass in my parish, accompanied by my dog. Whilst in Mass the dog always hopped into my seat, the driving seat, to wait for me. On that particular morning, while parking, I spotted a friend dropping off her daughter who attended the school beside the church. I walked over to her for a chat and a review of the latest gossip, but she was staring past me, her eyes round, her mouth half open. She was looking at my car moving slowly, the dog at the steering wheel apparently driving the car. A regular Mass-goer, who always wore a grey mac and carried two large bags, was walking into the car-park. She always regarded me with the sideways look of one who is scared, yet, fascinated by clairvoyance. On this morning she stopped short, dropped both bags, went bright red, then pale. Clasping her hands across her bosom she rolled her eyes upwards. 'Mother of the Divine, It's a miracle' 'The hand brake on my car has gone,' I explained to my friend. 'Leave it in gear, next time,' she advised, laughing, and drove off.

Very Special Powers

Earlier in the book I described a man who came to me for a reading to find out who stole his money. He was illiterate and had managed to make a great deal of money. I respected his loyalty to his family for he had preferred to know that the thief was the son of the woman he loved, a boy in whom he had placed a lot of trust, rather than the relative with whom he fought and argued. He showed a sense of family loyalty that I both like and respect, even though some people may not understand such a point of view.

The power I felt and had that morning were nothing to do with me and all to do with his own psychic ability, which I now recognise to be both extraordinary and extremely rare. At the time I tried hard to recapture some of that ability, to enter again into, another's world and life. It was a magical and unique experience. It was his power, not mine, that drew me into the breakers yard, and into the small wooden office overlooking it. It was that illiterate man's power that created for me the pictures I saw, all that I heard, and then the frightening, but exhilarating sensation of participating in person in the scenes I saw.

As a permanent feature of my clairvoyance I would not like it one little bit. I would be like a ghost drawn by psychic threads into other's lives and worlds, nothing but an unseen observer, helpless to alter anything. I much prefer what happens to me now when I get vivid but fleeting pictures and sounds, to aid what I see in the palms or cards. It is hard enough when I am searching for a missing person because then I have to evoke much deeper psychic abilities. I need to track a person on what is often their last journey, enter into their thoughts on leaving this world. That is very, very demanding because I feel what that person felt and it is not always a peaceful sensation.

For days, and sometimes weeks afterwards, the sight and emotions of the family left behind stay with me. I am one with them, and feel all the burden of their sadness and loss.

Animal Magic

My brother has a lovely labrador bitch who was dumped on the family by some callous individual, and who subsequently became a great family pet. A litter of pups she had carried were all given away to good homes and she was then subject to the minor surgery to ensure that she would not have any more pups. After this she moped and brooded for a while, but became even more attached to my brother's children who all love her. She is affectionate and always comes to me when I call to the house. A few days after my son died I was at my brother's house and the bitch came up to me as usual. Then she stopped a few feet from me, shook herself, and turned and walked away. I called her, she hesitated, as though trying hard to approach me, could not, and this time walked out of the house. This showed me, more than anything else, that animals do have an awareness of human emotion, and an awareness of events that have taken place. When she did eventually return to me for a pat I felt genuine comfort.

A friend's daughter in Florida is very attached to her miniature dachshund and believes that in a former life he was a person whom she loved. She wanted me to give the dog a reading. I thought it nonsense but I am very fond of the girl and agreed, to humour her, to give the reading.

I was amazed at what the cards turned up, for they formed into the same sort of story pattern as do cards when I read them for a person. What was startling was the behaviour of the dog. He hopped onto the girl's lap, put his paws on the table and looked at me with so much intelligence in his brown eyes that I was sure I was relating to a person.

'And in his previous life he was evidently very intelligent and well thought of,' I said as part of the reading.

At this point he sighed, as though deeply satisfied, and laid his head on his paws, still watching me with that alert intelligence. At the end of the reading I said, 'I can't see anymore for now.' On cue, he looked away, jumped down, and waddled away to his biscuit cupboard. There he stood, his tail wagging stiffly in the air and an expression on his face saying, 'I've been a clever boy and deserve a biscuit.'

A magical place and a delightfully magical experience.

Chapter Nine

Are You Psychic?

If you have had any dreams foretelling future events, strongly intuitive feelings about another person, a vivid sensation of liking or disliking a place on entering it, or just plain curiousity about the future then the answer is yes, you are probably psychic. There are degrees of psychic ability and developing this ability takes time, patience, and a lot of practice. The ability to focus the mind and develop powers of intense concentration takes a great deal of practice and effort. Once other people know that you are training yourself to develop your psychic ability it can have some pitfalls, so be warned!

I was at the races with a few friends, enjoying the sort of day out I love. The strong wind was fresh carrying the scents of the turf, the horses, the charcoaled steaks, and the sound of drumming hooves flying at the finishing post. A very smart woman with rather piercing eyes kept looking at me. Her look was so obvious and intent that I felt I should know who she was, so I kept trying to think where, or if, I had met her.

It seemed as though I could not go to the parade ring, the tote, or to the loo, without seeing this woman staring at me. Despite that we had, a good, wind-blown day, broke even financially, and ended with ravenous appetites at a hotel near the race-course, sitting down to a good dinner. Across the restaurant, at a table with a man and two children, was the woman who had so fixedly looked at me all afternoon. Now she was staring even more intrusively, and I began to feel a vague sense of persecution.

'Don't look now,' I began to the friend beside me. That is

fatal of course, because it invites *everyone* to stare in the same direction at the same time. 'But there is a woman at a table over there, near the mirrored wall, sitting with a man and two children. She's wearing a cream silk suit and has black hair. Do you know her?'

Everyone turned simultaneously, looked, then looked back at me shaking their heads .

'Don't know her from Adam,' was the consensus of opinion.

But the woman got up after a few words with her companion, and walked over to our table. Her cheeks were flushed and her expression agitated.

' You've been watching me all day, reading my mind. You've just told these people something about me! Stop it! It's driving me mad – I know who you are, I saw you on television!'

She would not wait long enough for me to assure her that nothing of the sort had happened, and that I had found her intense scrutiny unnerving and irritating. However, I know very well by now, that it is a belief that people hold onto. They really believe that psychics are mind readers, and are at it all the time.

Focusing the Mind

Try concentrating on a single item or picture, keep your mind on it for a few minutes. Inevitably in the beginning your mind will wander on to other things, but you must train your mind to stay with the object on which it is concentrating. It is the reverse of all our training and upbringing, that is what makes controlling our own minds so difficult. We are trained to think ahead, to associate one thing with another, to allow our minds to run on. For example when teaching a child the time we point to five o'clock and say, 'That is tea-time'. From very early on we learn to think of Monday as beginning the week, a day of work, and Friday as closing the week. Sunday is associated with rest, and with religion. We do all our important learning by association. Therefore any meditation, or mind focusing, is difficult because it requires us to reverse all we have been trained to do.

Suppose you have decided to concentrate on a postage stamp. You are perfectly still, warm and comfortable, your mind is clear and alert. You can see the stamp very clearly in your mind's eye. Then you see the envelope and on it an address. The letter is addressed to a friend, or relative. Next you think of that person and what you might have said in a letter to them.

So the natural process of thinking by association has begun. Often people give up at this stage believing that they will never master the art at all. Do not give up, stay with it. There is a simple technique to reverse this process. Instead of forcing your mind to return to the postage stamp, in one leap, re-trace your steps backwards in your mind along the thought path that led you away to begin with.

If you started thinking of the stamp and ended up thinking of a friend or relative in Australia, then start with the person in Australia and work backwards through all the thought stages that took you away from the first object of your meditation or mind focusing exercise. If you keep on doing this you will, I promise master this most difficult and elusive of all arts.

Psychic Type

While anyone can build on what skills or talents they already have, I do believe that there is a psychic type that can be recognised from their physical appearance. The eyes are often green or hazel. The expression in them often seems piercing, mesmerising. This expression often shows on a person's face – in their eyes – after practising meditation. There is a restlessness in the manner and all five senses are sharp and alert. Psychics often complain of fatigue while appearing to have a great deal of energy. Psychics often do not feel the cold and radiate great body heat. If you know that you fall into that category, have already had strong premonitions or actual extra-sensory perception, then it is well worth your while persevering with the exercise in mind focusing.

Acting on a Hunch

It has many names; a hunch, premonition, intuition, sometimes it is a fleeting feeling, at other times it is such a strong feeling that it drives us to activity that we would not normally undertake. Even if the intuitive feeling is mild, hardly noticeable, allow it to grow. Examine what the feeling is prompting you to do, then examine all the factors around it. Say, for instance, you get a very strong feeling to ring someone up and while you are looking for the number that very person rings you. That often happens. We call it telepathy, or sending thought messages. We regard it as something very special. In fact what happens is that we are reminded of the other person by some word, event, piece of news, common to both. And if you think back to something on the news on radio, television or in the newspaper you will spot what that was.

If you get a really strong urge to visit a relative or friend and, on getting there find that something is wrong with the person, you will thank your mysterious hunch for bringing you on the journey. But, if you think rationally there might have been something in the other person's appearance, or something that they said, that registered in your subconscious mind and then your subconscious mind, knowing the appropriate moment to act, sends out a signal to the body and conscious mind. When you learn to trust your subconscious mind, it will send through more and more information to you.

Eye-Power

There is nothing like plain observation. Watch how a person moves, sits, gestures. A restless person will always take a seat near the door, no matter where they are, at home, in church, at a dinner party. That is not clairvoyance, that is just plain observation. Observe what kind of person wears a particular sort of colour. Learn to develop personality relationships in this way. The more you practice the easier it will become.

Cards

Get any book on the meanings of cards, read it, take what you can from it, then practice, practice, practice. Earlier in this book I said that I began by laying out the cards on one day of the week and checking back a week later to see what had happened, thereby measuring the cards and my own reading of them against events occurring immediately after putting out the cards. By this method you will not be able to see something occurring in the coming weeks or months. It is limited, but it is a useful and easy way to start.

Palms

Pester all your family and friends to let you look into the palm. If you start with people you know then you have the advantage of knowing a great amount about the person's personality and history. By looking at several people with the same sort of hand you will find out what sort of things they have in common in terms of personality and life-history. That way the meanings of the shape, length and markings of the principal lines will become clear.

Why?

It is all a lot of hard work, learning, and concentration. If you want to develop your psychic powers you must be clear as to why you are doing it. If it is for fun that is not a bad reason at all, because it can be a lot of fun. If it is to help or entertain other people, that is a good reason. It does help people, it also fascinates and entertains them.

But if you are doing it for yourself, to know more about your own future, forget it. Apart from being able to interpret your own dreams as a guide to future events, you will find, as I have found, that you cannot do readings for yourself. They simply do not work out or make sense. Pity, is it not?

Chapter Ten

Psychic Power

Everyone who comes to me for a reading does so in the confident knowledge that whatever we discuss never goes beyond the room in which the consultation takes place. The only time I ever broke this self-imposed ruling was when I learned that a woman who had come to me for a reading had subsequently told her friend that I advised her to sue the friend. I shall call the woman Jane, it is not her name, but will do for the purposes of this illustration. Jane is an accountant and is friendly with a family who own horses. Apparently Jane rode one of her friends horses and fell sustaining an injury. She claimed that all this was discussed at her reading and I had seen in the cards that she should sue for damages which the court would certainly award.

'How could you have told her such a thing?' Jane's friend demanded. 'Jane has an injury, but she didn't get it falling from one of our horses.'

Although I did not say what had been discussed in Jane's reading, I assured the friend that there was no question of my having given such advice. I am not sure if she believed me, but I did at least try to redress the matter.

In this chapter I want to describe three particular and different uses of psychic power. To do this I have asked the permission of the three people I name and discuss and they have agreed to have their stories told.

Beauty and Death

A stout girl in her late teens came for a reading. She had short black hair, clear olive skin and shrewd dark eyes. I had an instant and vivid impression of her bending over the face of a dead person, she seemed to be tending it. There was no impression of grief, only of tranquillity. I was curious and interested. Her hands were rather square and well shaped. The palm lines were deeply grooved. The line of life was long and curved, showing good health and a sensible approach to life. The line of heart was delicately curved and showed someone who had the ability to love, but might on occasion be shy and conceal tender feelings behind a gruff, or jocular mask. Her head line was fascinating, it showed someone with the will and ability to make a success of a business of her own.

I commented on this and the girl nodded determinedly. 'I would like to make a go of a business.'
Her lines showed patience and persistence, as well as real brains, I had no doubt that she would succeed in her chosen field. Her cards showed that she had just completed, successfully, a course at college.

'I did a business course at the Regional College in Letterkenny.'

Still I could not find any sign of recent death to explain my impression of her bending over the face of a dead person. I explained what I had seen and asked her about it.

'My name is Pauline and my father is an undertaker in Donegal, I sometimes help my mother, to lay people out.'

'Is it the family business you want to go into?'

She frowned. 'I had always thought so. Right up until recently. Now, I'm not so sure. That's why I'm here, really.'

There was another business in her cards, a family business, that she might enter, although I felt then that undertaking would suit her very well.

'We farm as well, but I'm not interested in going into farming.'

There was a fine star shaped network of lines under the third finger of her right hand. This means real artistic ability.

When I pointed this out to her, she burst out laughing.

'I couldn't draw a straight line.'

I got an impression of great sensitivity from her hands, the ends of her finger tips were slightly pointed showing the ability to work with fine precision. I was puzzled. There was some very obvious career path here, but it eluded me. Again I had the impression of her bending over a still face, scrutinising it, professionally. It convinced me that she should enter the undertaking business, she had the head for business, and the ability to do such a difficult and depressing job with tact and sympathy.

Then I caught a faint scent of perfume, the face I had seen psychically was not a dead face but a living one.

'What about the beauty business?'

She smiled and looked enthusiastic. 'I had been thinking of something like that. Do you think it would work for me?'

I thought that any business Pauline put her heart and soul into would work, and nodded.

Her next reading was a year or so later. She had embarked on a course of training, but the cards showed that there would be more courses to follow over the next couple of years, the work experience she needed to gain professional status would have to be unpaid, and she was in for a long, not too well paid, haul before getting established.

'I don't care. I love the work, it's right for me. I'll do whatever I have to get trained and established in the business.

The determination in her face and voice was reflected in her palm lines. They glowed, and there were a few feathered lines developing along her head line showing intense effort and will power. The star shaped artistic lines were much more vivid now, an indication that she was using and developing her artistic ability. There was another line, only faintly present before and not much stronger. It ran from her life line across her head line and touched on her heart line. She had chosen a career for which she was ideally suited and one in which she would become successful and well known.

I had often thought it a pity that such a young and pretty girl was so stout, but it never seemed to worry Pauline at all, she was too involved with her career.

When I next saw her she had some very good work experience behind her and was ready to start a business of her own. Her cards showed the black aces and seven of clubs, a property contract on the way and one that could be quite smooth although it might only be a temporary move. She would be moving again within a couple of years to another business premises.

There was heat from her life line and a vaguely agitated buzzing. 'Are you well at the moment?'

She laughed. 'I'm finally getting around to dieting. The next time you see me I'll be three stones lighter and have long dark hair and, she looked very, very determined. 'I'll be making a go of the business in Dublin.'

The last time I saw Pauline she had a trim and graceful figure long dark hair and the quiet professional manner of the expert beautician.

She had never really needed psychic readings, only a little guidance and some reassurance from time to time.

Quest For Truth

Mary Anne is a gentle woman in her early forties. She has pale fair skin bright clear eyes and a shy and charming smile.

I sensed great sadness from her, a well of grief that was bottomless. Her first cards were the seven and eight of spades the cards of depression. They were followed by the ace and nine of spades, the cards of death.

'Has someone close to you has died recently.'

'My son, Paul, was killed in a car accident and I can't come to terms with it or get over it.'

There was such despair in her soft voice that I decided that this was to be a counselling session rather than a psychic reading. We were silent for a while, I waited for her to speak. People often come in grief and they want to talk, not be talked at, or, much worse, talked out of their feelings, or advised to look on the bright side. If there is a bright side to death, I do not know of it. It is a painful and wretched business. To bury one's own child is against nature. Yet, she was silent, watching me waiting for me to say something.

I looked into her palm and got an immediate shock. Her lines were at complete variance with her appearance. There was a fork at the base of her palm showing someone with exceptional powers of investigation and analysis. There was also an immense anger. This is usual in bereavement, but in Mary Anne's case, I felt that it was far more than anger because her son was dead.

Her head line, heart line and life line were all strong, remarkedly so, and all radiated anger and tingled with questions she wanted answered. Her cards showed that, besides depression, she felt isolated from other family members.

'They are not able to talk much about Paul.'

The cards showed that other family members did care, and very, very much but were not able to talk about the death. They each coped in their own way. And for some people that means in silence. We discussed this and she agree that this was so.

'Is that what makes you so angry?'

She shook her head. 'Not at all. I'm angry because my son should never have died. I think he got medication he should not have had at the hospital he went to.'

After a few minutes in tears a great rush of words came from her.

'Everything is wrong. He had a slight accident with his arm, he had some drink taken as he'd been at a twenty first birthday party. But I have the feeling that he was given something that caused him to crash the car.'

Helpless anger, the need to find a scapegoat, are a natural part of the grieving process. I hoped that such feelings might burn themselves out in Mary Anne, as the gradual and painful acceptance of her son's death took place. But the palm lines were strong and glowed with an angry determination to find the truth. There was a short line under her head line, she needed the truth.

'I don't know what I can do,' she looked at me in appeal. 'I don't have the education to fight this one on my own, and no one is giving me answers.'

Despite that she wrote countless letters to the hospital, to the government, to solicitors. She discovered that her son had been given medication at the hospital and that the side effects of such medication in conjunction with alcohol certainly meant her son should not have driven his car home from the hospital.

A solicitor she consulted told her she would need to put £10,000 up front before he would even agree to handle the case.

At this stage she wanted the matter sorted out in court. Mary Anne was determined to raise the money and to bring the matter to court. Some bereaved people take great comfort in such activity because it makes them feel that they are doing something positive and not simply accepting the whimsy of a very cruel fate.

By now many people were counselling Mary Anne, myself included. It was bordering on obsession and getting in the way of healing and acceptance. But she felt driven by the need to have the truth made public.

'What truth is it you want made public?' I asked her.

'That the casualty doctor should have tested Paul to find out if he had alcohol taken before prescribing medication. If he had then Paul might not have crashed his car on the way home and he'd still be alive.'

The cards showed conflict and that after a hefty and long drawn out legal process someone might be found to have acted erroneously. But it would not bring Paul back to his family. Eventually Mary Anne agreed to ask Paul directly for guidance in the matter. She took the cards, a look of intense concentration on her face as she dealt them. Her question was, 'Should I continue with the legal action.'

She put the cards down and cut them once. The ten of spades showed at the top of one pile and the ace of spades showed at the top of the second pile of cards. A clear and quite categoric, no.

She was disappointed but her real strength of character has shown in her acceptance of the advice given by the cards. She had felt guided by her son Paul.

Family Deceits

Grace now lives in Australia but I first met her in Bristol when she wanted me to read her cards to see if she was going to have a healthy pregnancy. She had masses of curly red hair, a freckled face and green eyes that twinkled like those of a naughty schoolgirl. She was twenty-four then, had been married for two years and this was her first pregnancy.

Her health cards showed the two red sevens on either side of the ace of hearts.

'You're expecting twins.'

'I'm big enough,' she patted her four months pregnant stomach, ' but I can't be having twins, there are no twins that I know of in the family.'

At the base of her index finger was a line, splitting into two, a sign of twins.

'I'm sure you're having twins,' I was emphatic. 'There are twins in your hand, too.' I looked at the start of her life line and got a buzz like an electric shock. 'You're a twin and I think your twin sister is also pregnant.'

Grace looked cross. 'I told you, there are no twins in the family. Mum and dad died a few years ago, but I know all the family, and there aren't any twins. You've got me all wrong.

I had a strong impression that Grace had a twin sister who was identical to her, but said nothing. Something was being concealed. There was a row of knaves across three eights, concealment and deceits.

The rest of the reading was quite straightforward. Grace and her husband were moving into a new house on the outskirts of the city, a house in which they would be very happy, but probably not remain in permanently.

' That's true. Keith wants to go to Australia or Canada. He can't see himself making much headway in the aircraft factory and we want a good life.'

Twenty years ago many people were emigrating to Australia.

Grace came back to me after her twins were born. She was a radiant and capable mother, in love with her husband, and happy in her new house 'We are definitely going to Australia, but that's not why I'm here. I did have twins, as you predicted. 'What I want is to get to the bottom of the business of me having a twin sister. Could you have been wrong?'

'Yes, Grace. I do get things wrong, and I could have been mistaken in what I felt.'

She looked at me shrewdly for a long minute. 'But you don't believe that do you?' I shook my head. 'Tell me what you can it doesn't matter to me, one way or another, but I'm curious.'

'We could start with your mother. Do you have a photograph?'

She produced one from her bag. 'This was taken about a year before mum died.'

Although there was a striking resemblance between the woman in the photograph and Grace, I felt that this was not her mother. I wrote the name, mother, on a piece of paper and held the pendulum over it, thinking of Grace. The crystal pendulum moved quickly in a clockwise direction.

'Your mother is still alive.' Grace drew in her breath very sharply, but she looked neither angry, or surprised. 'I had begun to wonder,' she began slowly. 'My eldest sister is very upset about Keith and I going to Australia. When I told her what you said about me being a twin she looked scared, and I thought she'd laugh. She's always been very good to me, especially after mum died we got very close.'

I looked at the cards, they showed Grace's mother, to be still a relatively young woman, of medium colouring and married with teenage boys. When I described this to Grace she was quiet for a few minutes.

'That's a description of my eldest sister Muriel.'

'Could she be your mother?'

Grace shrugged. 'Anything is possible, isn't it? I'll ask her outright. But what about the other thing you said, about my having a twin sister? I really want to know about that.'

'Ask your eldest sister if she is your mother, then ask her if you have a twin.'

Grace's sister admitted that she was Grace's mother, and that she had been born when Muriel was only sixteen. But Muriel flatly denied the existence of a twin and would not discuss the matter at all.

Grace and her husband decided to get on with their lives and go to Australia as planned, even though she felt there were dozens of questions she wanted to ask Muriel.

I got a telephone call from her a few months later. She had gone to collect a friend from the airport and while waiting at the barrier had watched her double walk through from a plane. The two women had looked at each other, quite stunned, before bursting into tears and embracing. They were identical twins.

The sister's name was Connie and she had been to England in a fruitless search for her natural mother who had given her at birth to her father's family who had brought her up until he married and could take her into his own home.

'Do you mean that my, sorry, our father is alive?' Grace could not believe it.

'No. That's why it was important to me to try to find my natural mother. Although the woman dad married is more than a good mother to me no one ever told me I had a twin.'

There were many remarkable coincidences the twins discovered about themselves, and they now share a loving and close friendship with each other.

I have had many surprises in my clairvoyant career, but Grace's story is the one that stands out most clearly in my mind as a fascinating and unusual one.